J.-Edmond Roy

In and Around Tadousac

J.-Edmond Roy

In and Around Tadousac

ISBN/EAN: 9783337193737

Printed in Europe, USA, Canada, Australia, Japan

Cover: Foto ©Andreas Hilbeck / pixelio.de

More available books at **www.hansebooks.com**

TO THE REVEREND JOSEPH LEMIEUX,

Parish-Priest of Tadousac.

I know a house with white walls and mossy roof, that is hidden away beneath the quivering foliage of ever-green beech and fir trees. The clematis and the nasturtium climb about it, mingling their variegated tints with the more sober green of the hop and the ivy. In the walled garden grow wild roses and *sweet smelling hay*. There is no luxury there; severe simplicity reigns around: it is one of those tiny nests dreamt of by philosophy as a fitting home for its votaries, and on its threshold may be read: *Parva domus, magna quies.*

This little house is the presbytery where dwells the parish-priest of Tadousac.

It was there, while enjoying a sweet repose, that I first thought of writing these humble pages.

I dedicate them to him whose guest I was for one day of my life and whose fellow student I was for ten years.

TADOUSAC

I

Arrival by night. – First sight of Tadousac. – The Mamelons. – Origin of the word Tadousac. – L'Anse à l'Eau.

It was eleven o'clock at night when our steamer touched Tadousac wharf, for its course along the Saguenay had been retarded by the heavy fog.

A smoky coal-oil lamp threw a lurid light on the deserted shore and the sleeping echoes of the solitary landscape woke to life on our arrival. From out the dark night there arose a most unholy confusion of noises, the captain shouting his orders to tighten the ropes, the steam engine laboring and panting, the trucks, for landing the mails, rattling and creaking. Suddenly shrill and powerful voices rose even higher than the already deafening turmoil and broke on the ear from the right, from the left, from above, from below. At one moment they seemed to issue from the very sides of the boat, at another to be borne on the crests of the waves, to spring from the thickets of dwarf firs, from the very beach itself. The stroller by night who stirs up the muddy waters infested by swarms of venerable old frogs could not awaken more dismal sounds than that indulged in by the Tadousac coachmen. For it was these gentlemen who aroused the passengers from their sleep by their piercing cries of Tadousac Hotel! Tadousac Hotel!

We had hardly entered the hotel coach when we found that we were crossing a tottering bridge of planks at full gallop. The elder ladies screamed with fright, whilst our Jehu, in a thundering voice, exclaimed to us: *It is very black tonight. If you see where you are, you be frightful.* Evidently this distinguished coachman who so jauntily sported his seedy old coat must have been a native of the place. We made him talk and he told us that there had been very few strangers that summer and that things had been going on very badly.

Nevertheless great expense had been gone to, the hotel had been newly done up and the servants were first-rate.

There were but about forty boarders in a large hotel which could conveniently take in some three hundred. The greater part even of these were transient boarders, being the wives of gentlemen who were away fishing on the upper Saguenay. He specially mentioned a poor lady, a millionaire, who every day when the sun was at its height was carried down to the shore in a hand chair. All this was very sad, but since we were seeking tranquillity, this state of things just suited us, for it enabled us to take a couple of days of real rest.

> We'd wander'd to the cliff's extremest edge
> And from this vantage-ground of rocky ledge
> The fierce, rude majesty, th'horizon bold
> Of the sad Saguenay we could behold.
> The night was falling and the fading light
> Threw solemn shadows o'er our eerie height

Sweetly and faintly did we hear the sound
Of the St Lawrence waters, ocean-bound,
Passing from sight into the distance drear,
Black Saguenay's deep waters rolled near
Bathing the feet of those tall world fame'd capes
Whose shadows darkly fall, whose mighty shapes
Stand out like tow'rs of fabled mystery
Guarding the Saguenay's dark artery
The traveller-laden steamer lay in sight
The lanterns shedding round a blood-red light
Which, like a gorgeous crimson banner's hue
The scintillating waves gave back to view
Heav'n's blue arch bedeck'd with many a star
Above our heads stretch'd infinitely far
A fairy dome above the estuary.

The above is a slightly free translation of the following lines composed by Fréchette, the well known Canadian poet :

Nous étions parvenus sur un coin de falaise
Véritable balcon d'où l'on pouvait à l'aise
Contempler dans sa fière et rude majesté.
Du morne Tadoussac l'horizon tourmenté.
Du haut de ce plateau, dans cette nuit tombante
L'ombre était solennelle et la scène absorbante ;
Ici, le Saint-Laurent qu'on entend bourdonner
Vaguement, et qui laisse à peine deviner
Ses lointains vapoureux noyés dans les ténèbres.
Là, le Saguenay noir, avec ses pics célèbres
Qui, jetant des flots d'ombre opaque aux alentours,
Semblent comme un amas de fabuleuses tours
Pleines de je ne sais quel farouche mystère,
Dressé là pour garder la ténébreuse artère.
A nos pieds le bateau bondé de voyageurs,
Dont les fanaux, hissant leurs sanglantes rougeurs,

Thus sang our Canadian bard one evening when the moon found him in a waking dream.

Alone and listening to the sea shore's songs *

But every one is not a poet, and, being belated travellers, we thought it would be better for us to await the morning before paying our court to the beauties of sleeping Tadousac.

To make use of the classic Fénélon's poetical expression, Tadousac has " a view expressly made to please the eye ". Nestled in a hollow of the steep Laurentides, it seems like a nest of verdure surrounded by bleak and barren hillocks.

The plateau on which it stands is on one side bordered by the great river whose waters dash incessantly against the rocky shore ; on the other, by the black waters of the Saguenay which gently die away as it were in a bay that is

---

Ainsi que des reflets de la brûlante oriflamme
Dans la pénombre, au loin, font brasiller la lame
Et puis, par-dessus tout, un beau ciel étoilé
Faisant cintre d'azur de points d'or constellé.
Comme un dôme féerique à ce sombre estuaire

* Seul, et prêtant l'oreille à la chanson des grèves

carpeted with sand of such **unrivalled** fineness and softness that no other shore can bear comparison with this one.

The bay itself is of so perfect an oval in shape that one might **well** fancy some mysterious artist had traced its outline on purpose to make a **contrast** with the **rude** outlines of the surrounding peaks which seem to have been roughly hewn **out with** hatchets.

We are three **hundred** miles from the sea and forty leagues **more must** be passed before we can reach Quebec. The river is here twenty four miles wide, and, across its dark blue waters, we catch sight of the line of mountains on the south shore and **can** perceive the roofs of the Cacouna and Rivière-du-Loup houses glistening in the sunlight.

Away in the St-Lawrence itself may be seen the rocky shores of Red-Island (Ile-Rouge), fertile **in shipwrecks**, and the flat shores of Hare Island (Ile aux Lièvres), both islands looking very **much** like ships at anchor. On calm days, **when the sea is like a** mirror, these islands seem to be springing from the bosom of the waters and to remain suspended in the air.

To the right are the gorges of the Saguenay, a strange sort of estuary or arm of the sea, an abyss hollowed out between two chains of barren mountains where only a few stunted birch and pine trees grow and which river is so wild and dreary-looking that one American writer has called it " the river of death " ; whilst another, more classically and less gloomily disposed, has compared it to the rivers Styx and Acheron.

"This river is as beautiful as the Seine, almost as rapid as the Rhone and deeper, in many places, than the sea " wrote a Jesuit missionary of former times. It is even said that its impetuous torrent sensibly affects the St Lawrence at low water and even at the distance of many miles is powerful enough to change the course of ships (1). Before venturing to cross it, Jacques Cartier waited a whole night at anchor under the shelter of Hare Island.

---
(1) Bouchette

"Having a favorable wind and the tide being half high," Champlain wrote (1), "on account of the Saguenay currents which might drive you in another direction, raise your anchor and set sail, double Cow Point (Pointe aux Vaches), your sounding-line in your hand always, have two or three boats at hand so that, having doubled Cow Point you can get yourself out of the currents of the Saguenay, if it is calm, and thus enter the said port......

"Being in the port, carry a good anchor to land, stick the wing of the fluke of the anchor well into the sand, place a piece of wood over the wing and have at hand some piles which you can thrust deep down in the sand to prevent the vessel from dragging its anchor. The land winds are to be feared. They come from the Saguenay in squalls which do not last long, but are violent and impetuous."

For a long while this river was fabulously represented as a sort of monster that devoured

---

(1) 1092-3 Laverdière.

TADOUSAC   13

such mariners as were bold enough to venture on it. It was said to be filled with eddies and to be subject to dangerous tempests and whirlwinds. Fishermen's boats were said to have been caught by gigantic waterspouts and pitilessly crushed against the inhospitable shores which were steep, shelterless and harborless.

The trading companies that had been established here contributed to keeping up these legends, since they wished to monopolize this immense territory.

For the last sixty years people have got over all this alarm and the mysterious river has been brought into subjection. Everything about it is known now except its unfathomable depths. In many places it has been sounded to the depth of 330 fathoms and yet no bottom has been found.

The Bay of Tadousac lies on the left shore of the river. The old writers have repeated one after the other that it was a good-sized port where twenty-five men-of-war could take shelter. The capacity of this bay has been greatly exaggerated and, at the most, five or six moderate sized vessels could anchor there, and we ourselves have seen in it nothing larger than coasting schooners. At nightfall or when the wind blows too fresh from the offing, these vessels put in and take on board their provision of water. Other vessels again cast anchor in Water Creek (anse à l'eau), a fine little creek separated from the main bay by a narrow peninsula. The passenger steamboat lands tourists in this creek. The Government has constructed a quay here and keeps it in good order, bestowing special attention on it on the eve of election time.

These two harbors are well protected against the tempests by the high, round-headed, breast-shaped hills which shut them in to the north. The winds most to be feared are those that blow from the river, but when the long Lark flats (batture aux Alouettes), which terminate the Saguenay shore, are not covered by the sea, they form a powerful bulwark.

Tadousac owes its name to the hills which

surround it, and was thus called by the Montagnais Indians who resided there (1).

No words can paint the calm tranquillity of Tadousac. The hamlet is only frequented by lovers of peace and quiet, whilst those, who are in search of a spot where they can let time slip away leisurely, need have no fear of being here molested by the intrusive idlers who frequent more fashionable watering-places.

The cliff itself offers every advantage for seclusion from intruders, since it abounds in little cosy, sheltered nooks whence magnificent views are to be obtained. The waves break at

(1) According to Mgr Laflèche the Cree or Indian word was *Totoushak*, plural of *Totoush*, nipple. Others again pretend that Tadousac is derived from the Montagnais word *Shashuko*, *Place of Lobsters*. This etymology appears to us as unlikely to be correct since the above mentioned *sea cardinals* are rare on those shores. According to the Jesuit Father Jerome Lalemant (in his lation 1646), the Indians sometimes called the port *Sadilege* Thevet, in his work *Grand Insulaire*, writes *Thadoyseau*.

The English write the word Tadousac; the French call it Tadoussac, and this latter way of spelling the name is to be found in all the old M S. The large modern dictionaries give both *Tadoussac* and *Tadousac*.

your feet, the shore is lovely, whilst pure water and good bathing are to be had at will.

Tadousac offers great advantages also to more sober-minded tourists who are in search of the unknown, as well as to the pale antiquary who would fain investigate obsolete forms of civilization and explore whatever ruins his wandering steps may lead him across.

This was the corner of the earth where the French founded their first establishments on Canadian soil. This was the centre whence the first missionary Jesuit Fathers went forth to convert and civilize the regions of the Saguenay and the mysterious North. One after the other the waters of this bay have been visited by the adventurous embarkations of Cartier, the discoverer, the swift, light barks of the Basque and Breton flibustiers, the ships of Chauvin, Pontgravé and Champlain. This was the first port entered by the French colonists before their arrival at the rock of Quebec, and it was from here that Druillettes, Dablon, Albanel, set out for the distant shores of Lake Mistassins and Hudson Bay.

II

Why Tadousac not a large city.- The Indians of prehistoric times.

Tadousac, Stadacona, Three-Rivers, Hochelaga, were for a long time the four great trading posts of the colony. Tadousac, the oldest, the richest, the most frequented, has remained stationary and is still nothing more than a miserable scattered village. The other three have grown to be populous centres. Tadousac, on the borders of two great rivers, the natural discharge of a vast hunting region, the first port that was entered by the European ships that were sailing up the St. Lawrence, was admirably situated for a trading post, but so soon as the wild animals of the North had disappeared through their incessant capture, Tadousac became once more what it had been : a wild country spot surrounded by mountains and precipices. Commerce or trade is as sensitive as the magnetic needle, as capricious as a barometer ; it is shifting and erratic. It is only **agriculture** that makes a people and builds up **large cities.** Champlain well understood this **when, against the** opinion of his associates, he **deserted** Tadousac and founded Quebec at the foot of the rock of Stadacona. Champlain had **to contend all his life with** the companies of grasping merchants, who snatched the tools from the hands of the few colonists he had been able with great difficulty to get together, forbade **the** workmen to sell their produce to any one **but those** in these said companies' employ, to **buy elsewhere** than in their shops, or to traffic in any way without their permission. Champlain in spite of all these difficulties founded a great **country,** where his name has been always held in honor, while the names of Monts, Pontgravé and Caën have fallen into oblivion.

During a century the Basques covered the waters of the **Gulf of** St. Lawrence with their **venturous** barks. They disappeared, like the **whales** which they had pursued, without leaving any trace except that their names had been given to some few desert and unknown islands. The same fate has befallen all the receiving houses or factories dotted about the north coast of the Lower St. Lawrence: Port Brest, once so well known, **Fort Pontchartrain,** the trading posts of Mingan, St-Modet, Seven Islands and many others whose names even have now escaped from memory. The sea, tired of yielding up its treasures, has flowed back again over the fortunes won from it.

The fur-trade had spread far and wide the fame of Tadousac.

Let us try to describe what this trading village was like, for formerly it was famous, and it has pleased geographers, writing from the seclusion of their studious homes, to class it among the large cities.

The vast territory to which, in primitive times, was given the name of the kingdom of the Saguenay was inhabited by a dozen or so of savage Indian nations, scattered and nomadic tribes, living on the produce of their chase in the woods or on the great lakes. These Indians were designated generally by the generic name of Montagnais and are a part of the great Algonquin family. They were not all of the same blood, nor did they speak the same tongue, but having united against the invading nations of the south, their long alliance had led to their having the same manners and customs. It is the instinct of self preservation that causes the homogeneousness of nations.

The narrow strip of land that stretches along the banks of the St. Lawrence from Murray Bay (Malbaie) to the little islands called Jeremiah (Jérémie) was the domain of the Tadousacians. The tribe of the Betsiamites was on their left and separated them from the country inhabited by the Esquimaux, a strange sort of race who have never taken kindly to Christian civilization.

Proceeding up the river Saguenay, on nearing Terres Rompues, might be seen the first wigwams of the Chicoutimians. These latter had taken up their quarters on the peninsula which has retained their name. Behind the heights of the western bank of the Saguenay lived the Little Mistassins and the Papinachois. The former were a branch of the Great Mistassins whose hunting grounds extended northward to the still undetermined region of Lake Mistassini, an immense inland lake or sea, where our ancestors had establishments, but where we have not yet had the courage to penetrate. The word *Papinachois* signifies *ever smiling* and the gentle and sympathetic nature of the little tribe bearing that name has been ascribed to the whole Montagnais branch of Indians. On the confines of the Papinachois territory lived the Ounescapi in a country so miserable and so inaccessible that it is only about thirty years ago that the missionaries succeeded in visiting this tribe for the first time. The bold traveller who could penetrate unharmed into the sombre marble cavern where the Great Spirit dwelt at the head of Lake Mistassini reached the tribe of the Ouchestigouets, then that of the Cariboo People (Gens du Caribou) and the Otter Nation, (Nation de la Loutre) the last region that was washed by the waves of the North Sea (Hudson Bay).

Having passed beyond the Chicoutimi peninsula we come on the Pickougamians, a quiet modest people whose light canoes plough the tranquil waters of Lake St John. And, in a westerly direction, above the Ahsapmouchouan cataracts rises the encampment of the Chamouchouanists and the huts of the Indian fishermen of lake Nikouba.

No trace of government or of civil or religious laws is to be found among these tribes. They were dispersed by the sea-shore, along the rivers and lakes of the interior or in the depths of the forests whence they procured their nourishment. The waters of the sea and the lakes yielded them plenty of fish, the woods gave them plenty of game of various sorts. They delighted in taking their food half-raw and they slept on the mossy beds or on the sands of the shore. Around them was the primeval forest. They gathered from it a few evergreen pine tree branches to ornament their dwellings. The flexible bark of the birch tree furnished them with clothing, utensils, material for their swift bark canoes, and everything wherewith to construct their habitations.

The Iroquois and Hurons, inhabiting the fertile plains to the west and the south, were stable, stationary nations. They built villages which they fortified against their enemies; they tilled the ground and gathered in a goodly harvest of Indian corn. The Montagnais were not husbandmen. In the winter they wandered through the forest in groups consisting of two or three families, staying their course wherever they met with good hunting. The summer always found them on the water-side at Tadousac, Three-Rivers or Quebec. They would there subsist on smoked moose or what fish they caught. If they came to a fruit tree they would cut it down in order to gather the fruit. (Rel. 1633). They were tall, straight, strong, well proportioned, agile, and had nothing effeminate about them. No nation under heaven was droller or fonder of joking and fun. Their life passed in eating, laughing, bantering each other and jeering at the neighboring tribes,

They were thoroughly "good fellows." The Hurons were professed thieves and like the Spartans of old taught the trade to their children. The Montagnais, on the contrary, prided themselves on their disinterestedness.

The Hurons and the Iroquois had regular forms of government. It is said that the former were governed by women, the latter by old men; which quite explains the inconstancy and levity of the former as well as the ambition and astute policy of the latter. The Montagnais leading a nomadic life had no need of a stable government. However they gave themselves war chiefs or captains, whom they obeyed when it pleased them to do so. Some of these chiefs obtained the command by right of birth, others by being elected to it. For example, if the son of a captain managed well and was naturally eloquent, he succeeded his father without any opposition. In order to pay a tribute of honor to the virtue and courage of a renowned chief, the nomination of his successor would sometimes be deferred for several years. It was usually the relations of the deceased chief who named his successor. When the day of election arrived, the candidate was stripped of his apparel and the family of the deceased chief replaced this by new garments. It was the family of the deceased also who feasted the electors and finally the dead chief's wife crowned the newly elected one who thereby assumed even the very name of his predecessor (1).

These chiefs possessed a more or less fictitious power, but it was not the same with the fortunate Indian who had distinguished himself by the bravery he had shown during some encounter with the enemy. This latter assumed great airs of consequence and became really a ruling power, under the name of war-captain. The Tadousac war-captains have always had a high reputation and history has recorded the names of many amongst them. Later on we shall see how one of them, by an alliance contracted in a most unexpected manner, has left his mark on the commencements of the colony.

Like all nomads, the Montagnais looked

---

(1) Relations of 1669 passim.

down on other nations and prided themselves on being the only nobility of the country, for had they not the most splendid hunting grounds in the world for their domain? Thus these undisciplined men, who apparently took no care about anything, were for a long time the dominating race, attaining to this distinction either by means of their alliances, or through the numerous offshoots of their tribe that had been planted in the most distant forests, by their wandering groups of hunters.

The Montagnais had made Tadousac the favorite centre or great summer station of all the northern nations. From north to south, from east to west, all the Indians assembled at Tadousac. It was there that the most beautiful Canadian furs were traded for, and among these furs it was the marten that held the first place.

The canoes of the Nipissings and the Temiscamings, of the Round Heads (Têtes-de-Boule) and the White Fish (Poissons Blancs) approached this shore side by side with those of the Micmacs, the Abenaquis and the Etchemins.

They bartered beaver and otter skins **for arrows.** The Hurons brought meal, **Indian corn** and **tobacco which** they exchanged for deer skins.

Such were the various tribes who inhabited the mysterious Saguenay and the environs of Tadousac at the time that Cartier first landed on its shore.

Jacques Cartier. — The establishment founded by Champlain. — The Court of King Petault. — Champlain. — The Basques, hardy seamen. — Their smuggling trade.

It is in the relation of his second voyage of discovery, made in 1535, that Jacques Cartier speaks of the Saguenay as a " deep, narrow river of very dangerous navigation." Having cast anchor at its mouth, he was nearly losing his galley (1). At the time of the St Malo navigator's expedition in 1540, he had received express orders to explore this mysterious river, where, according to the information furnished by the Indians who had been taken to France, there were to be found " great riches and a very fine country (2). " Cartier had no love for this Saguenay shore " this rock without any savor

---

(1) Cartier's voyages ed. 1843, p. 29.

(2) ibid p. 70.

of earth" which he thought had been bestowed on Cain by God, and therefore the task of visiting it fell to Roberval. The latter proceeded there in 1543 with eight barks manned by 70 seamen One of these barks foundered in the Saguenay waters and eight of the expedition were drowned (1). Among these eight were Sieur Noire-Fontaine, and a man named Levasseur from Constance. Roberval's pilot, Jean-Alphonse le Saintongeois, who accompanied him, returned back convinced that "this river comes from Cathay, for in that place a strong current runs, and a terrible tide rises (2)."

To reach Cathay, by crossing the American land, was the dream and ambition of all these hardy pioneers of the sea.

There exists no detailed account of this voyage made by Roberval. According to the version which Hakluyt has given of it, the exploring party that left France-Roy on the fifth of June returned at the end of about nine days

---

(1) Roberval's voyages p. 96. Pinkerton.
(2) Le Routier p. 84.

It cannot be supposed that in so short space of time Roberval could have penetrated as far as to the head of Lake St John, as some authors would have us believe. Again, what sense can there be in the ridiculous story so gravely related that Roberval never returned from his Saguenay expedition and that in all probability the vestiges of an old entrenchment that have been discovered on the borders of the Mistassini point out the spot where he perished (1)?

On the arrival of Champlain, Tadousac emerges from its first infancy, and the legends surrounding its cradle vanish from sight. Champlain relates to us how de Pontgravé of St Malo, merchant, who had long been trafficking for furs with the Canadian Indians, formed the project of establishing a monopoly of this trade. In order to aid him in putting his project into execution he fixed on the captain of a Norman vessel, Sieur Chauvin. This man, who thoroughly

---

(1) Osgood's *The Maritime Provinces*, ed. 1883. It has been proved that in 1544, a year after his Saguenay voyage, Roberval was in France.

understood navigation, had powerful friends at court where he had a certain influence through the services he had rendered during the late wars. Chauvin obtained the exclusive privilege which de Pontgravé had solicited, on condition of inhabiting the country and founding an establishment there. These two men embarked at Honfleur in 1599, accompanied by several artisans and others, and they landed at the port of Tadousac. De Pontgravé wished to commence an establishment higher up the St Lawrence, but Chauvin decided otherwise and chose to establish the base of his operations at Tadousac. He had a house built there four fathoms (1) long, three wide and eight feet high, which house was covered with planks and had a chimney in the middle. It was built like a guard-house, surrounded by hurdles and a trench dug in the sand (2). A little stream

---

(1) *Champlain's Works* p. 699. Chauvin's habitation is marked on Champlain's map of Tadousac (1608).

(2) A fathom is 2 yards.

ran lower down. They left sixteen men to pass the winter there. When their people " were made warm and comfortable for the 'winter," Chauvin and de Pontgravé returned to France. The winter coming on, these poor forsaken men soon learned the difference of temperature between France and Tadousac; it was, says Champlain, like the court of king Petault, where each one wanted to be head. Idle and discouraged, they soon ate up the provisions that had been left them; they were scourged with illness and they would have died of starvation, had not the Indians taken them to their own cabins. Eleven of them perished miserably. This first experiment did not discourage Chauvin who in 1600 pursued his traffic with good results. In 1601 he was about to finish his year's campaign, an equally profitably one, when he was seized at Tadousac with an illness that sent him to a better world.

From that time forth, the reputation of Tadousac spread abroad. Lewis Roberts, in his *Commercial Dictionary* printed in London, in

1600, relates that the port of Brest on the Labrador coast **was** the principal post of New France, the residence of a governor, an almoner **and** several other officials ; that the French brought thence great quantities of cod, of **whalebone** and whale-oil, as **well** as beaver skins and other valuable furs. He adds that the French also kept up a fort at Tadousac, in order to trade with the Indians for peltry. **The " Relations "** and various travellers spoke a good deal about Tadousac and the geographers, from their writing tables, pronounced it to be a town. Some authors, Abbé Langlet du Fresnoy, for instance, even set forth that there was jurisdiction established there. All these exaggerations succeeded in exasperating Charlevoix. "The greater number of our geographers," he says, (1) " have marked a town at this port, but there has never been than more one French house and a few cabins belonging to Indians who came **there** at the trading-season and who afterwards

---

(1) III vol. p. 65.

carried off their dwellings, as people carry off the booths after a fair."

The Basque, Norman and Breton sailors contributed in no small degree to spreading the fame of Tadousac. From time immemorial these hardy mariners, braving the unknown ocean, had fished on the banks and coast of Newfoundland; for centuries before the illustrious pilot of St Malo first landed on the shores of the St Lawrence, coasters from Bayonne, Dieppe, Honfleur, Havre de Grace and La Rochelle had visited these regions in pursuit of whales and also walruses, monster cetaceous animals, of which the seals of our days are but degenerate and bastard descendants. These men had even given names to many of the ports they frequented before captain Jacques Cartier ever touched at them, writes Lescarbot. "The great profits," says the commentator of the *Jugements d'Oléron*, "which the inhabitants of Capberton" (Cape Breton) "near Bayonne, and the Basques of Guienne realized from the whale-fishery, and the facility they acquired in it, decoyed and enticed them to become so venturous that they sought these animals all over the ocean in all the longitudes and latitudes of the world. For this purpose they formerly fitted out vessels in order to go in search of the haunts of these monsters. It was thus that, a hundred years before Christopher Columbus crossed the ocean, these mariners had discovered Great and Little Cod Bank, (Banc des Morues), Newfoundland, Capberton and Baccalaos (which in their language means cod), Canada or New France, where there are many seas abounding in whales."

In fact, Cartier recounts that even so far as Canada many whales, porpoises and sea-horses are to be found. Charlevoix tells us that being on board the *Heros* in 1705 and having anchored at Tadousac he saw there four whales which were nearly as long as the vessel. Also, all the old historians write that the Basques met with great success in capturing these cetacea in the waters that bathe Tadousac. They left traces of having dwelt there in various places

A little lower than Green Island (Ile Verte) is Basque Island (Ile au Basque), where, in the time of Charlevoix, might still be seen the remains of ovens and whales' ribs. In the Magdalen Islands too there is a Basque Harbor, (Hâvre au Basque.) Champlain and Lescarbot (I p. 214) report how the Basques went whale-fishing with the Escoumains in a creek which bears their name. About twelve miles above Tadousac may also be met with Cape Basque (Chafaut aux Basques). Lastly, it was the founder of Quebec himself who gave the name of New Biscay to the magnificent basin formed by the Beaupré Hills (Côte de Beaupré), the entrance of the river St Charles, la Canardière and Cape Diamond (Cap Diamant). La Potherie says: "In the river there are a great number of whales. The Basques had a permanent fishing-ground there some years ago, and, had they not amused themselves by secretly carrying off all the pelts from Tadousac and its environs, they would not have subsequently found themselves deprived of their property."

Commerce attracts commerce. The whale-fishery had attracted the Basques to the **Gulf of St Lawrence**, but in their adventurous expeditions, having **met with** Indians, they commenced to trade with them for furs, always a precious commodity, for they saw in this traffic a much more ready and profitable way **of** enriching themselves **than** by continuing their whale-fishery. Their traffic **had been free and** uncontrolled until the arrival of **de Pontgravé**. The establishment of a monopoly was not likely to find favor in the sight of mariners accustomed to the freedom of their roving life.

Tadousac was at that time the rendezvous of the nomadic tribes of Canada who, every spring, hastened there to meet the Armorican and Breton mariners and barter **away to them** their beaver and marten **skins**. The Saguenay marten was already held in great esteem by European nations.

The customs of centuries cannot be changed in a moment. A serious conflict therefore nearly **arose** in 1608, **when** de Pontgravé, **on** returning **to Tadousac**, announced **to** the **Basques** that they **could no** longer **trade** with the

Indians without first obtaining the privilege of so doing from de Monts, who had inherited Chauvin's monopoly. The Basques under the command of captain Darache, an old whale-fisher, little accustomed to the restrictions imposed by letters-patent, fired unceremoniously on de Pontgravé's vessels, wounded two of his men and killed a third. They were about to spike the guns of the intruder who had come to disturb them in their operations, when Champlain arrived. More diplomatic than de Pontgravé, Champlain concluded an armistice with the insurgents and it **was mutually agreed** to refer the settlement of the dispute to the **king. Two** years afterwards, in 1610, the rumor having spread in the French sea-ports that the **king** had rescinded de Mont's privileges, the greed of the merchants for beaver skins was so **great**, says Lescarbot (1), that three quarters of **them**, thinking to get the golden fleece without striking a blow, did not even succeed in obtaining woolen fleeces, so great was the number

---

(1) Book V, chap. V.

of competitors. Champlain, for his part, tells us that there was so great a number of ships at Tadousac that there was but little trading. Many, he adds, will long remember their losses. However, this unfortunate year did not discourage any one. In 1611, Tadousac was still covered with snow when three ships cast anchor there. The chronicler says, that, by arriving the first, they hoped to reap ampler profits, but the Indians awaited the arrival of more ships in order to buy and sell on better terms. " Thus those people were mistaken, remarks Champlain, who thought to do great things by arriving the first : for the natives are now too cunning and clever. "

The Basques, being cut off from trading, organized a smuggling campaign which they continued to carry on most actively on these shores until the commencement of the 17th century. In 1613, Champlain arriving at Tadousac publicly read out his commission and gave orders that the king's arms and letters-patent should be attached to a post in full view of the public, so that no one could plead ignorance of them. Sieurs de la Moinerie and la Tremblaye, although promising to conform to these orders, continued to trade away their merchandise for the pelts furnished them by the natives. At one time Champlain would surprise La Rochelle vessels in giving the Indians " a quantity of firearms, with powder, shot, tinder, things most pernicious to place in the hands of these infidels who might make use of them against us some time or other. " At another time it was the Spaniards who went to Tadousac in order to spy out the company's transactions. The smugglers from La Rochelle and elsewhere had, at that time, their post of observation on Green Island (Ile-Verte). In 1621, de Caën and de Monts fitted out a vessel in the port of Tadousac and went in pursuit of them, but, says Champlain, the birds had flown two days previously. All that remained was an intrenchment of palisades. This was at once burnt. From the time of the pilot Jean Alphonse, Green Island had already been called the island of war. And every year, under pretence of fishing for whales, the Basques, Spaniards or Normans managed in some way to exchange their merchandise for pelts.

IV

Champlain meets the Indians.—How an unfortunate alliance grew out of a visit of courtesy.—The founder of the colony as a theologian.—The first one to break his pipe.—The brothers Kertk.—The death of captain Daniel at Tadousac.—His funeral.

Champlain arrived, and, as we have said, tore aside the veil concealing the origin of Tadousac. In fact he was the first historian of this *terra incognita*, and no one has spoken better of it than he. His descriptions are always so faithful and so exact that on perusing them Tadousac is easily recognized.

Such as Tadousac then was, such is it at the present day. Let us open Champlain's journal at the page recording the day when he entered the harbor of Tadousac, May 24th, 1603, and read what he says:

"Tadousac is a small bay, at the entrance of the river Saguenay, where there is a current of water and a tide most remarkable for its swiftness and depth, and where, at times, there blow violent winds, causing great cold. This port of Tadousac is small and could only hold some ten or twelve vessels ; but there is plenty of water to the east, sheltered from the Saguenay river, along a little mountain almost on the borders of the sea. Besides this there are high mountains, where there is but little soil, but plenty rocks and sands where grow woods of pine, cypress, fir and several sorts of trees of little worth. There is a little pond near the said port, shut in by mountains covered with wood. At the entrance of the port there are two headlands : the one to the west stretching a league into the sea, called St Mathieu or Lark Point (aux Allouettes) ; and the other, to the southeast, projecting a quarter of a league, called Point of all the Devils, (1) so named from its great danger. The S., S S B, and S S W., winds blow straight into the port. Point St Mathieu

---

(1) Now called Cow Point (Pointe aux Vaches.)

and Point of all the Devils are nearly a league apart ; both of them are dry at low water. "

All the historians since Champlain have copied from him, but none among them have had his powers of observation or his correct eye. The short description, which he gives of the Saguenay after having gone up it for about fifteen leagues, can be read more than once. How exactly true is what he says of "this land of mountains and rocks, the greater part of which is covered with woods of fir, cypress and birch, a most unpleasant sort of land, a regular desert uninhabitable for animals and birds." With what astonishing exactitude again, with nothing to go upon except the simple accounts given by the Indians, did he trace the itinerary of the mysterious depths between Tadousac and Hudson's Bay.

From 1603 to 1631, Champlain chronicles the principal events of this distant post, a daily chronicle always enlivened with typical details. One seems to be living the very life led in those primitive times. The scenes which he describes in so naïve and charming a style, are so life-like that we feel more like having been ourselves actors in them than we have in now being mere posthumous spectators of them. On closing the book the reader is astonished at having travelled so far, in so short a time, and without any fatigue.

This Point St Mathieu which I see yonder fading away into the somewhat misty morning horizon, I remember having approached in a little Biscay boat rowed by four vigorous boatmen, and having there landed on a little rising shaded by cypress and fir. I remember calling to mind the superb reception given to Champlain, May 27th 1603, by the great sagamo Anadabijou, surrounded by about a hundred Indians, and how the interpreters, his fellow countrymen, related to him what they had seen in France: the splendid chateaux, the palaces, the power of the great king who was sending him aid against the Iroquois. And the great sagamo and his warriors brandishing the skulls of the enemies they had just vanquished in a great fight, after having danced and smoked for a long while, offered to Champlain a superb feast of Canadian elk venison. It was on this Lark Point, during an impromptu feast, that was consummated that alliance between the Algonquins and the French, which was to exercise so great an influence on the destinies of New France. In good deed, this tongue of lonely land was a witness of one of the most important political events of the French era. A most decisive step was here taken, for it was here that was concerted the plan of the great struggle with the Iroquois, which commenced that long campaign which was to cost so much blood and so many sacrifices to our ancestors. One might almost think that a strange destiny had so willed it that on the shifting banks at the Saguenay's mouth, the date of the first French establishment in Canada and that of the death-warrant of the colony should be inscribed side by side. (1)

(1) No reliance should be placed on guides like Osgood who place this scene of 1610 at Pointe Boule and speak of Lescarbot being present at the great council, whereas he had not then ever been in Canada.

And on the morrow of this crossing of the Rubicon, I see the Indians embarking in their light canoes "made of birch-bark strengthened inside by little hoops of white cedar," then landing in the sandy creek of Tadousac. They are coming as diplomats in old Europe might have done, to return the visit which Champlain had made them.

One of their chiefs is chanting a long wailing song in the style of Ossian's verses. He recounts the deeds of valor and prowess of the last campaign, the number of enemies who bit the dust, their valor and their misdeeds. Homer could not have better sung those deeds. The old men, seated in a semi-cercle on the shore, from time to time interrupt the orator by guttural sounds equivalent to hear! hear! of our own days. At each verse the women and the girls, with dishevelled hair, perform a frantic dance, letting fall some particle of their clothing at every step, so that at the end of the "complaint" they are as slightly clothed as the fair Amphytrite issuing from the bosom of the waters. The furious passionate dances of the classical

Bacchantes were not to be compared with the strange weird evolutions performed that day on the Tadousac sands.

This carnival having ended, the penetrating and serious mind of Champlain rose to higher considerations. He felt uneasy about the souls and the religion of these children of nature. Heretofore when the king had given the monopoly of the Tadousac trading to Chauvin, Champlain had deplored that this speculator was of the " reformed " sect. It was interesting to listen to him, questioning the sagamo Anadabijou.

The latter, in all confidence and simplicity, explained to him his ideas as to the formation of man, how God, after having made a number of arrows, stuck them into the ground, whence there issued men and women.

Champlain, on his side, would relate the Bible tradition concerning the creation of Adam and Eve, speaking of the unity of God and the mystery of the Trinity.

The Indian, after having listened to him meditatively, after a while continues :

He had heard say that in olden times five men going towards the setting sun met God face to face and he asked them: Where are you going? We are going to seek our living, replied the five travellers. And God said to them you can find it here.

The travellers passed and God, taking a stone, struck two of these obstimate men with it and they were immediately turned to stone. Where are you going? said he again, adressing the three remaining men? We are going to seek our living. Go no further, you can find a living here. They stopped a moment and, seeing that nothing came of it, continued their way. God then taking two sticks struck two of the travellers and they were immediately turned into sticks. The last man remained completely stupified. Where are you going, asked God of him? I am seeking a living. The example of his four comrades made him reflect a little. He stopped and listened to what God had to say and God then gave him meat and he had a very hearty meal.

On another occasion, continued the great

chief who had now become garrulous, God asked a man who had plenty tobacco where was his pipe? He gave it to God who after having smoked a good deal broke the pipe into several pieces. Why did you break my pipe? you see I have no other. And God took one which he had and gave it to him, saying: There is one which I give you, carry it to your great sagamo and tell him to keep it. If he takes good care of it, he will want for nothing, neither he, nor any of his companions. So long as he kept that pipe the Indians wanted for nothing. But one day he lost it, and from that time forth the Indians have suffered from famine.

The primitive inhabitants of Canada had no good cheer and scarcely any notions of good and evil except what referred to those two points. Perhaps, it is this story of the great sagamo's pipe which has given rise to the common expression among Canadians. *He has broken his pipe* (Il a cassé sa pipe), to indicate that a man has met with some ill luck.

Champlain, serious and grave, even while noting down in his memoirs the fables that were recounted to him by the Tadousac chief, does not forget to note down likewise the lessons from the catechism which he gave him in return.

All this higly displeases the sarcastic Lescarbot who maintains that the Bible traditions were quite incomprehensible to the Indians, even supposing that the narrators of them had spoken the language in perfection.

Before the king had given the monopoly of the Tadousac trade to individual companies, numerous vessels used to come and anchor in that port. An old man used to relate to Father Lallemant that he **had seen** as many as twenty vessels at a time (1). Bergeron, in his treaty on navigation, published in 1629, says the same thing. The " Relations " of 1626 thus recount the manner in which the companies, being jealous of their privilege, carried on their trade.

So soon as the trading was assured to the association, to the exclusion of all **others**, the

---

(1) " Relations " of 1626.

Relations says there were no longer more than two vessels to be seen and they belonged to the association. Even these were only seen once a year, at the beginning of June. These two vessels brought all the merchandise which the association traded away to the Indians, i. e., great-coats, blankets, night-caps, hats, shirts, cloths, hatchets, arrow-heads, awls, swords, instruments with which to break the ice in winter, knives, iron pots, dried plums, grapes, Indian corn, peas, biscuits and tobacco. In exchange the Indians brought the skins of the Canadian elk, the lynx, the fox, the otter, the marten, the musk-rat, but principally the beaver which was the most prized. In one year alone 22,000 skins were shipped. Generally the cargo consisted of from 15 to 20,000 at a pistole each*. The company employed forty persons and more, whilst the crews of the two vessels numbered 150 men. All these had to be fed and their wages paid, so that the expenses were considerable. Some of these men had 106 livres;

*Ten francs make a pistol.

others 100 livres. An interpreter had 100 pistoles, as well as a right to a certain number of skins.

It may well be imagined with what anxiety the Indians awaited the arrival of the vessels every spring. So soon as the snow melted, they arrived at Tadousac, and for long days together, standing in groups on the loftiest summits, they looked to the horizon. As soon as a sail was sighted, bonfires were lighted at the Point of all the Devils, and the more eager among the Indians hastened to their canoes and went far out into the river to meet the vessel. Clothed in bear skins, all disguised and hideous, were they with their noses painted blue, their eyes, eyebrows and cheeks painted black and the rest of their faces painted red, for such was the grand full-dress which they assumed for the occasion. The large vessels would remain anchored before Tadousac while the barks would continue their way up to Quebec and Three Rivers in search of pelts which they brought down to the principal station. The year that Champlain had laid the foundations of the capital of New France, he had commenced a habitation at Tadousac. Not a single vessel went up the river before having anchored in this harbor. It was there that de Pontgravé and his assistants passed the winter when the necessities of his trading made it advisable. Quebec was then only a pied-à-terre or temporary place.

For nearly twenty-five years, one company had succeeded another in the lucrative monopoly of Tadousac amidst divers vicissitudes. Chauvin had died, leaving his powers to de Chastes. De Monts and de Caën had succeeded them, quarelling over the booty whenever they had some respite from the Basques, who were hardy contrabandists.

Champlain exerted his great powers of conciliation to try to make peace between these two grasping traders. The port of Tadousac beheld more than one acrimonious scene between the crews of the rival traffickers. Called on to arbitrate between them, the "father of the colony would not allow himself to show any preference for the one or the other, since he had to do justice." So as not to be an eye-witness of de Caën's acts of violence he tells us how, on one occasion, he preferred going up the Saguenay.

When their common enemies, the Basques, were overcome, or when the manner of dividing the profits of trading had been settled, there arose questions of religion between Huguenots and Catholics and these were by no means the least perplexing subjects of disagreement.

During the summer of 1628, David Kertk' a Dieppe apostate, who had gone over to the service of the English, undertook to reconcile the discordant parties by taking possession of Tadousac where he burnt all the privateers and broke up the mill-stones which de Caën had negligently left there instead of sending them to Quebec. "They would have been as well at Dieppe as at Tadousac, remarks Champlain, for what could we do with them there?"

The following year Kertk returned to the charge. It was from Tadousac that he sent his two brothers to Champlain summoning him to give up the fort of Quebec. The little garrison forgotten by the traders, half-starved, with nowhere to look for succor, laid down their arms and their conqueror sent them to Tadousac. Kertk, elated with his easy victory, had a tent put up adorned with verdure and, in this tent surrounded by his captains, he celebrated his victory.

The Kertks had formerly been wine-merchants at Bordeaux and Cognac and knew nothing of the sea. They had been brought on this expedition by a French deserter, captain Jacques Michel, a Dieppe Huguenot. Displeased at the Kertks taking to themselves all the merit, he was threatening to take from them what he had procured for them, when he suddenly was seized with a great drowsiness. After having been thirty-five hours without speaking he gave up his soul, most fortunately for the Kertks but not so fortunately for himself, if, as Champlain does not doubt, he went to hell.

" I left my country, he said to Champlain, and did wonders to serve a foreigner; never again shall I be happy for I shall always be held in horror by every one. I have no hope of returning to France where I have already been held up to reprobation. Since I am thus treated on all hands, I am driven to despair and forced to do worse deeds than I have ever done before."

This wretched man, says the Relation of 1634, had, on the eve of his death, uttered terrible blasphemies against God and against St. Ignatius, declaring that he wished he might be hung if, before the next evening, he had not given a couple of slaps in the face to one of the Jesuits who had been captured by the English, at the same time using most injurious language concerning the Father. He was soon after taken with a malady which rendered him unconscious and of which he died like a dog the next day. The surgeons, of whom there were a great many, did not treat him rightly, for they gave him sleeping-mixtures when he was already in a state of lethargy.

Michel's character was violent and irascible and he had already had a very animated quarrel with the Jesuit Father Brebœuf at the port of Tadousac. One day, David Kertk had thus addressed the Jesuits : " Gentlemen, your business in Canada has been to enjoy the property of Mons. de Caen whom you have dispossessed of it."

Excuse me, sir, replied Brebœuf, we came here from pure love of God, and we have exposed our lives in every way for the sake of converting the Indians. "

" Yes, yes, of course, for the sake of converting the Indians, but you really mean converting the beavers, exclaimed Michel.

" That is untrue, said Brebœuf.

" Michel raised his hand as if to strike him : But for the respect I owe to the general I would slap your face for having given me the lie.

Brebœuf, who was of herculean proportions kept cool : " Excuse me, said he, but I did not intend giving you the lie ; I should be very sorry to do so. It is an expression that we make use of in our schools, when a doubtful question is proposed to us, and we take no offence at it, therefore I beg of you to pardon me and to believe that I had no intention of offending you."

The Father's excuses did not calm down Michel and his anger was so great that some people say it caused his death.

The death of this unhappy turn-coat gave more pleasure than it caused regret; nevertheless he was buried at Tadousac with all the honors due to his bravery and his rank. Louis Kertk had a coffin made for him wherein the body was placed, and a drawn sword was laid on the cover. Two hundred men at arms landed from the vessels in order to escort the mortal remains which were carried on the shoulders of the marine officers. At the head of the cortege marched a man fully-armed bearing a round shield and a cutlass, and a blackened pike was broken and thrown on the coffin. When the corpse had been lowered into the grave and the minister had said the last prayers, the soldiers fired two volleys, whilst 90 guns were fired by the vessels which were anchored in the port (1) and had their flags at half-mast high. As soon as the ceremony was finished, every one returned on board. "The mourning did not last long, adds Champlain ; on the contrary never was there more rejoicing, **principally on board one of the vessels, where there were a few barrels of Spanish wine. He was thus paid out for all he had done.**"

After the departure of the English, the Indians dug up poor Jacques Michel's body and treated it with the greatest indignity. They hung it to a tree and, after having cut in pieces, gave it to their dogs to eat. (2) " Behold the reward of traitors, I pray God to open the eyes of the others, adds **Father le Jeune**, after having recounted these abominations. " (3)

In 1631, " The Company of One Hundred Associates " (Cents Associés) fitted out another

---

(1) The vessels were anchored at Moulin Baude and they gave themselves the trouble af going to Tadousac in order to bury him. (Laverdière.)

(2) Relation of 1634.

(3) Relation of 1632. Many writers have confounded captain Jacques Michel with one of the brothers Kertk.

vessel for the Tadousac trade, but the fear of meeting with the English made them put in at Miscou at the entrance of the Bay des Chaleurs. The following year, the king of France took definite possession of the colony, and the traders continued their trafficking relations with the Tadousac Indians.

V

The Tadousac trading.—Trading post.—Of the king's farming out of the trading and the sub-farmers.—Surveyor Normandin's explorations.

From the period of the French re-taking of the country until that of the final cession to England, the trade of Tadousac passed through many phases. At first, the various companies had the monopoly of trading. As soon as the navigation was open, their vessels hastened from France to Tadousac, in search of the pelts that had been collected at the different posts dotted along the river and which had been brought there by various barks. In 1645, after having battled for it a long time, the colonists obtained free trading. Having formed themselves into an association under the name of "The Community of the Inhabitants." (La communauté des habitants,) they took the direction of the Tadousac factory or receiving house. In 1648, the trading at this post gave 40,000 livres*

* A *livre* is worth nearly a franc.

profit and the total amount or value of their transactions was 250,000 livres. There were 22,400 pounds weight of skins exported, without counting 500 elk-skins. Each spring the frigate belonging to the "Community of Inhabitants," visited Tadousac. Bissot, Bourdon, de Tilly, Godefroy, Repentigny. Couillard de Lespinay, were among the principal directors of the Community. In 1653, a Dutch freebooter, armed with sixteen guns, penetrated to these shores in order to trade with the Indians.

The Company of One Hundred Associates, (Cents Associés), who regretted having conceded so many privileges to the colonists, had sent out an active, persevering agent, who commenced to watch the **commercial** operations of the community closely. An advocate, connected with the Paris Parliament, Peronne de Mesnil was crafty and had as much penetration as a detective-officer. He ended by accusing the directors of having 644,700 livres unsecured. As those on whom fell the blame of **this were** the first people of the country, **they** employed violence to make him **withdraw his accusations. His** papers were seized and **he** had to embark **for** France. The memorial which Peronne de Mesnil presented to the king still exists. It is violent and aggressive, **but** unfortunatly the documentary proof which ought to have accompanied his statements **is** not now to be found, if it ever existed.

It became customary to sell the privilege of trading at Tadousac at public auction. The money realized **by** this sale went to pay the expenses of keeping up the colony. We find, in 1653, a deed of partnership concerning Tadousac trading between Louis Couillard and Messieurs Rosée, du Hamel and Co, represented by their agent, Germain Le Barbier. On October 19th, 1658, a decree of the Superior Council of Quebec adjudged the post of Tadousac to Sieur Demaure. In 1663, **Governor** d'Avaugour thought proper, on his own private authority and contrary to the custom, to confirm this privilege for two consecutive years to the following seventeen individuals: de la Tesserie, des Cartes, Le Gardeur, Gourdeau, Le Gardeur de Tilly, **Desprez,** Juchereau, de la Ferté, Bissot,

Damours, Charron, Madry, Marsollet, Le Gardeur de Villiers, Chartier, P. Denis, Bourdon and Juchereau de St Denis.

This displeased the inhabitants very much. In their petition to the Council they pleaded that Mons. d'Avaugour had no right to alienate this public property. Their complaint was looked on as just and Oct. 4th, 1666, the Council annulled the lease given by d'Avaugour. This decision, however, was of no advantage to them, the king having already, in the preceding month of April, disposed of the Tadousac trading in favor of the West Indian Company which had been formed two " years " previously. This new company was to enjoy their privilege in the same way as the " Community of Inhabitants" had been accustomed to do, that is to say, on condition of defraying the annual expenses of the country (1). In 1674 the company of the one hundred associates whilst giving up their monopoly, reserved to themselves the Tadousac trading until their final dissolution. For a mo-

---

(1) Ed. & Ord. t. I, p. 61.

ment the "Inhabitants" had hopes of once
more laying hands on this factory, for in 1675
we see that the Superior Council had intimat-
ed an order to them to assemble that they
might know how to dispose of it. This domain,
reputed to contain the best hunting and fishing
places of all North America, was never again
to fall under the control of the colonists. The
king took it back for his own benefit, first farming it out to Oudiette and his partners, and
afterwards every twenty years renewing the
lease to the farmers of the excise (gabelle) who
succeeded one another in France. From that
time forth the Tadousac trading, which includ-
ed the exclusive right of trafficking with the
Indians on the north of the Lower St. Lawrence, was known under the general name of
"King's Domain" (Domaine du Roi) and
became an integral part of the " Combined
Farms of France" (Fermes Réunis.)

    These farmers wished to make the most
out of the immense territory which had fallen
to them. Their claim extended even to the
south shore of the river. The inhabitants of

this region opposed such trespassing most energetically until the month of June, 1685, when their own right of trading with the Indians was recognized. These farmers too for a long time opposed all enterprises which in any way could damage their monopoly. In 1681, Frontenac refused permission to Radisson to establish trading-posts along the northern mouth of the St. Lawrence, for fear of their interfering with the Tadousac trade.

This country was always much prized by the contrebandists. In 1707, Raudot forbad every one, even the Indians from elsewhere, to trade or hunt within the Tadousac limits. In 1709 he renewed this prohibition, giving permission to the Tadousac sub-farmers to pillage the French who might be found "feasting the Indians" or trafficking with them. In 1701, and in 1720, these same severe orders were renewed.

It is worthy of remark that when the traffic of brandy was forbidden in the colony, under most severe penalties, it was allowed at the Tadousac post, although the trading there was under the control of the Government (1).

The large farmers did not always work alone, although they had a regularly appointed director of the domain in the colony to collect their dues or taxes. La Potherie tells us that there was a company of merchants at Quebec who annually paid a certain price for being alone allowed to trade with the Saguenay Indians (2).

The sub-farmers were numerous; Louis Bergeron had the lease of Tadousac for six years (3). Cugnet, towards the end of the French domination, traded to considerable profit at this post, according to Bigot (4).

In 1750, the widow Fournel farmed the Tadousac territory. Three years previously

---

(1) Letter of Aubert de la Chesnaye, Oct. 24th, 1693.

(2) Mons Marmette, in his reports on the archives of Paris, points out a memorandum of Mons Riverin dated Nov. 19th, 1685, in which he describes what the Tadousac trade really is, what is being done to destroy it and the means necessary to be taken to preserve it for the king.

(3) Collection of Quebec, vol. 12, 3rd series, 1731.

(4) Letter to the minister, Oct. 11th, 1749.

Hocquart informed the minister that no one had wished to farm this part of the district.

The limits within which the privilege of Tadousac trading were allowed to be carried on were for a long time a source of difficulty. Intendant Hocquart put an end to this in 1732. The preceding year, Pierre Cartier, General Contractor of the united farming of France, had demanded the authorization of his exclusive rights of trading, hunting and fishing, throughout the whole royal domain, from the Ile aux Coudres as far as two leagues below Seven Islands (Sept Iles) as well as in the dependencies of the posts of Tadousac, Chicoutimi, Lake St John, Nikobau, Mistassini, Papinachois, Naskapis, River Moisie, Seven Islands, including the lands and seigniory of Murray Bay (Malbaie) under pain of a 2000 louis' fine for all infractions. The Intendant, following the special instructions he had received from the king, gave orders to Aubert de la Chesnaye to make an exact survey and map of the domain, from below Ile aux Coudres to river Moisie as far back as it extended to the high lands and to draw up a report of his operations in the form of a journal.

Most detailed instructions were given to Mons. de Chesnaye in the form of a journal. Not only was he to take note of an immense territory and measure it, but he was also minutely to indicate the rivers that fall into the Saguenay, with the direction they take from their sources to their mouths, to mark how far they are navigable in ships, boats or canoes, the falls and rapids where portages or carrying places were had recourse to, the situation and extent of the lakes, the names of these lakes and rivers and the countries they crossed, the establishments and store houses where trading with the Indians was carried on, the seal hunting, the salmon fishing, the former establishments, where trading had been carried on and of which some vestiges remained, the names of the Indian tribes who inhabited these countries or frequented them for trade, their number and every thing in detail which could serve to specify the extent of these territories and make known their advantages.

Aubert de la Chesnaye set out on his mission **May** 12th, 1732, but having broken his leg at Little **River (la Petite** Rivière) when beginning his journey, the surveyor, Joseph Laurent Normandin, was appointed to replace him.

Normandin penetrated 200 miles to the **N. E.** of Lake St. John, **further** than any modern surveyor has yet done, and made the most faithful and detailed map of this region that we even yet possess. On this map we **can** see marked, 189 miles to the N. E. of **Lake** St. John, the establishment of a Mons. Pelletier which starts up unexpectedly amidst the solitude and the appearance of **which gives rise** to all sorts of fantastic suppositions. "Who was **this** Mons. Pelletier thus living alone in this distant and almost inaccessible region ? What strange design can he have **had,** asks **Mons. Arthur** Buies (1). Was he a trapper, a philosopher, a hermit ? No tradition enlightens us on the subject ; we must content ourselves with admiring the boldness and courage of a man who **was capable**

---

(1) Le Saguenay : Avant **propos** IX.

of living absolutely alone in such a state of exile, exposed to many dangers and feeling able to brave them all.

On May 23rd, 1733, Intendant Hocquart, basing his decisions on Normandin's observations, definitively fixed the limits of the Saguenay territory and trading grounds of Tadousac. The *King's Domain* (Domaine du Roi) as they then called this vast extent of ground, the superficies of which was at least 72,000 miles, reached from the lower extremity of the Eboulements seigniory to Cape Cormoran, below the River Moisie, that is to say, it was about 300 miles in length. A straight line drawn from each of these extremities toward the north is the demarcation of the eastern and western limits of the reserve. On one side were the high lands dividing the waters of the rivers St. Maurice and Batiscan from those which fall into Lake St. John; on the other side were the still unknown regions where dwelt the Naskapis and the Esquimaux. Twelve principal trading depôts were then in full operation within this network, of which Tadousac was the centre and the rallying-point. These limits are much the same as those indicated in the official order of 1658 bestowing the right of trading in Tadousac on Sieur Demaure.

To the east, a concession that had been made Feb. 28th, 1661, by the company of New France to François Bissot, Sieur de la Rivière, had already made a breach in the domain. At the solicitation of Cartier, the heirs Bissot renounced their rights to the portion of land extending from Ile aux Œufs to Cormoran Pt, four or five leagues below River Moisie. To the west, the seigniory of Malbaie had formerly been conceded to Mons Hazeur, but the latter had sold it back to the king at a good price (1). This seigniory was thenceforward united to the domain and was only detached from it after the Conquest. The extreme northern limit had always preoccupied the government of the colony. Several times had they sent to take possession of a certain portion of land, but the English who were trading at Hudson's Bay did

---

(1) 20,000 livres, title Oct. 29th, 1724.

not believe in renouncing their own claims. In 1713, the minister wrote to Mons. de Vaudreuil that he was certain the English would hardly give up Lake Nemiskau on account of their trade with Rupert's Land. He insisted on the necessity of keeping the Mistassins on account of the Tadousac trading. Lake Nemiskau and the Mistassins were retained, though there was some fighting about the tract of ground in dispute. This extreme limit which was then contested is still being contested to this very day.

In the mandate fixing the limits of the trading territory of Tadousac, Hocquart renewed the prohibitions made by his predecessors. He even went beyond them, for no one was to approach nearer than ten leagues to the confines marked out.

We here see with what jealous care the farmers of the domain protected their monopoly. No one had any right to pass over their lands except the government officials when on each change of farmers they were sent to value the buildings and furnishings of the posts.

The missionaries, however, had free entrance everywhere. It was very much to the advantage of the traders that the missionaries by the exercise of their ministry should collect the Indians in groups and thus keep them at a distance from the Hudson's Bay trading posts. In the spring of 1725, Mons. **de Tilly made** a voyage to Chicoutimi, but it was only **in** order to examine what woods were fit for furnishing masts for the king's navy.

In a book entitled: *Contest in America*, published in 1757, Dr John Mitchell declared that in N. America the French had **only right** to the rock of Quebec and **the** factory or trading post of Tadousac. At the conquest the rock **of** Quebec as well as the **factory of** Tadousac passed into the hands of **the** English. The king's domain remained a reserved spot adjudged to the highest bidder as it had been for a hundred years previously. **The farmers of** it continued to exclude strangers **from their** domain and to keep **hidden its resources**, **both** in order to keep up their monopoly and to foil all attempts at competition whenever the lease had to be renewed. This is why it is only fifty years since the Saguenay district has begun to be colonized.

In the larger Tadousac hotel, a few years ago, there might still be seen in the gardens the last vestiges of the buildings which had belonged to the old company of the King's Posts. They have disappeared, as have also disappeared the powerful traders and the Montagnais Indians who formerly met each other, at that post, every summer.

VI

The Tadousac missionaries. — Huguenots and Catholics. — Recolets and Jesuits. — One hundred and sixty-seven years of apostleship. — 1615-1782.

In the first charts there were two ideas that predominated, in the region granted to the French explorers of Canadian soil : religion and commerce. The idea of colonizing was an afterthought. For many, however, the conversion of the natives was but a pretext which served to mask their mercantile designs. Was it not, indeed, strange, to see the home government entrusting Huguenots with the task of spreading the true faith among these new nations?

Champlain terminates his recital of the first attempt to found an establishment at Tadousac and its miserable failure, by saying : That which was blameable in this entreprise was the giving to a man of contrary religion the commission of spreading the Catholic, Apostolic and Roman faith, which these heretics hold in horror and detestation. This is the fault I find with the undertaking.

The ephemeral vice-royalty of the Catholic commander de Chaste did not prevent the first traders from importing the lamentable old-world quarrels into the free land of America. De Caën's crew, partly Huguenot, partly Catholic, disputed for the pre-eminence in the port of Tadousac. When on board of his ship, de Caën made his co-religionists sing Marot's psalms in his cabin or on the poop, in the place of honor, whilst the Catholics were relegated to the fore part of the vessel which they shared with the common sailors.

This allowing the natives to have cognizance of these disputes was indeed a fine way of executing the king's orders to catholicize them.

Historians are not agreed as to where the first mass was celebrated in Canada. Mons. Louis Frechette, holding with an old tradition which speaks of this ceremony as having taken place on the spot where now stands the village of Tadousac, has written some fine verses on this subject in the **Legend of a** People (Légende d'un Peuple). We will let the poet speak for himself.

> And there, beneath the cool green shade,
> The parish temple rears its head
> On that same favor'd spot, 'tis said,
> Where on the altar, years ago,
> The Saviour's precious blood did flow.
> When, to the sound of pious song
> Borne by the echoes far along
> The mountains with the rounded crest
> Stretching afar from East to West;
> By Breton priest with whiten'd hair
> The sacrifice was offered there,
> Whilst, mid these scenes so wild and new
> Knelt Cartier and his hardy crew
> . . . .
> They who had come to win the land
> Are gather'd on the rocky stand,
> Far from their native shores, or dear,
> Encircled by the mountains drear;
> I think, I see then, kneeling there,
> Their heads are bow'd, their foreheads bare,
> Their clothes still stiff with ocean spray.
> And yet fervently these Bretons pray,
> Offering to him, now dwelling there,
> The holocaust of praise and pray'r.

As previously, the above is a feeble attempt to give a free translation of Frechette, the poet's lines. We here adjoin the original French :

Derrière nous, dans l'ombre, un petit sanctuaire,
Temple paroissial de cet obscur canton,
Dressait son humble seuil au lieu même où dit-on
Quelques cents ans passés, sur un autel rustique,
Pendant que le refrain de quelque vieux cantique
Etonnait les échos de ces monts inconnus,
Devant Cartier et ses hardis marins, venus
Pour arracher ces bords aux primitifs servages
Pour la première fois sur ces fauves rivages,
Un vieux prêtre breton, humble médiateur,
Offrit au Dieu vivant le sang du Rédempteur,
. . . .
Je vous revis, là, tous ensemble agenouillés,
Rudes marins bretons, dans vos sarraux souillés
Et raidis sous l'embrun des mers tempêteuses,
Au milieu de ce cirque aux croupes montueuses,
Au fond de ce désert, loin du monde connu,
Offrant à l'Eternel, tête basse et front nu,
Sur le seuil redouté d'un monde ouvrant ses portes
L'holocauste divin qui fait les âmes fortes.
. . . .

The first missionaries of the budding colony were Recollets. On May 25th, 1615, Champlain landed at Tadousac, bringing with him four of these religious, Fathers Jean Dolbeau, Denis Jamay, Joseph le Caron and the lay-brother, Pacifique Duplessis. The vessel continued to Quebec a few days afterwards and there the Fathers held council and decided on placing the Fathers in different parts of the country. Father Jamay remained at Quebec whence he served Three Rivers, to Father le Caron was assigned the Huron country where the French had not yet penetrated, and Father Dolbeau went to Tadousac to instruct the Montagnais and other Indian tribes as far as the gulf of St. Lawrence (1). They had a vast field : 350 leagues of country in a straight line.

Father Dolbeau, in December of the same year, went to Tadousac and there built himself a cabin with a kind of chapel attached so that he could assemble the French and Indians and perform the offices of the Church. He not only occupied himself with the conversion of the Montagnais, but he bore the gospel to the Betsiamites, the Papinachois and the Esquimaux.

Whilst Champlain was enlarging the field of American geography to the west, Father Dolbeau, says Garneau (2) was doing his missionary work among the Montagnais of Tadousac,

---

(1) P. Leclercq: *Etablissement de la Foi.*

(2) 242-1

and also traversing the mountainous and picturesque district of the Saguenay, to visit the Betsiamites and other Indian tribes to the north of the gulf St Lawrence. Many years afterwards, traces were found of his passage among these tribes (1).

On his arrival from France, in 1617, the Recollet Friar Paul Huet said mass at Tadousac, in a chapel made of foliage, whilst two sailors stood near him waving green branches to keep the mosquitoes away (2).

From 1618 to 1622, the mission of Tadousac fell to the share of Father Le Caron. A chief named Choumin adopted him as a brother and invited him to share his cabin. Choumin in French, *Raisin*, (grape) had received this name through his fondness for the juice of that fruit. He was also called *le Cadet*, (the junior) because he kept his clothes very clean and did

---

(1) La Potherie, p. 208-4.

(2) Parkman (*The Pioneers of France in the New World* p. 418) says that this was the first mass celebrated at this place. In all probability, however, Father Dolbeau must have said mass there at an earlier date.

his best to imitate French manners. He made himself useful to the missionary by helping him to give greater solidity to the house which the Recollets had commenced, on a piece of ground which had been given them the preceding year by the Company of Associates. His wife having presented him with a son, Choumin consented to the child being baptized on condition that he should be named Father Joseph. Father le Caron thought it best to conform with Choumin's notions of civility [1].

Parkman relates the fright experienced by the Recollet Father Gervais Mobier, when, for the first time, he saw a band of Indians dressed for dancing at Tadousac. He thought he had met with a band of demons. His fright increased still more when, having been invited to a banquet given to two hundred guests, he found himself in presence of four large pots filled with fish and pieces of bear flesh, the flavor of which was heightened with peas, prunes, figs grapes and biscuits. These messes were being

---

[1] Ferland, 203-4.

stirred with a small oar by way of skillet or ladle. As he did not seem inclined to do honor to the food set before him, his hosts tried to tempt his appetite by giving him a large slice of bear's-fat, a tit-bit usually reserved for great personages. The good Father could not manage it and had to give up the attempt.

The Recollet Father le Caron was the first instructor of the Montagnais. Understanding well the Indian languages, he had prepared studies in the Huron, Algonquin and Montagnais dialects which were presented to the king.

The *Relations of the Jesuits* take no notice of the apostolic labors of the Recollets in the Tadousac region and Father Charles Lallemant makes a mistake in saying, in 1626, that, during the ten years the Recollets had been living in the country, they had not been able to find an interpreter to teach them the Indian language.

This remark might give rise to the impression that the sons of St Francis had not commenced any mission work, for **want of sufficient** knowledge of the different idioms spoken in that region. It is, however notorious that, from the time of their arrival in the colony, the Recollets had resolutely set to work and **that they** were the first to bear the **tidings of** the gospel to the more distant **tribes.**

However this may be, the Jesuits whom the Recollets had summoned to their assistance, ended by replacing them. Before **they** had **even set** foot in Quebec an **abominable** pamphlet (1) had been **circulated from** house to house **in the** growing town, **in which** pamphlet the Jesuits were accused of **having** instigated Ravaillac's crime, when that fanatic killed

The only king whose memory is cherished by the people.

Four months after their arrival the *Anti-*

---

(1) *L'Anti-Cotton.*

Le seul roi dont le peuple ait gardé la mémoire

Cotton (1) was burnt by the hangman. The interpreters obstinately refused to instruct the sons of Ignatius in the Indian dialects, being impelled to adopt this course either through instructions to that effect having been given by the traders, or through their fear of seeing their own importance lessened. It was only, during the winter of 1633, that Marsolet, the celebrated Montagnais interpreter, yielded to their solicitations and imparted to the Fathers sufficient knowledge of the native languages to enable them to become masters in their turn. The Recollets, being an order that had no private resources, had never been able to do more than sketch out gigantic plans. The Jesuits, who were skilful organizers, and

---

(1) The Jesuit Father Cotton was Henry the Fourth's confessor At the time of that king's assassination the Father published an explanatory letter (lettre déclaratoire) concerning the doctrine of the Jesuits (1610), and defending his Order from the accusations made against them. This apology met with contradictors who published the *Anti-Cotton*, or *refutation* of the explanatory letter, in which they tried to prove that the Jesuits were the instigators of the regicide of Henry IV. Is it not astonishing to find this pamphlet disseminated in Quebec from the very first ?

had means at their disposal, fitted out vessels to bring out to the still feeble colony whatever could not otherwise be procured on account of the weakness or want of good will shewn by the companies.

The first efforts of the Jesuits were directed towards the far-off nations of the Lakes, amongst the Hurons. Although the Tadousac Indians were the first whom the French had met with when going up the river in their vessels, the good tidings of the gospel were only borne to them after having been preached to several other tribes (1). The good Fathers had foreseen that the centre of the future Canadian empire was to the West. Horace Greely's famous phrase is but a faint parody of an obscure missionary's idea.

The Tadousac Indians were nomads and the Jesuits considered that it was impossible to instruct them till they became stationary.

---

(1) Relations of 1641, p. 50.

" One cannot expect much from them until then, they wrote (1).

" Today we may instruct them, tomorrow hunger may force them to seek their living in the woods. If we undertake to follow them, we ought to have as many Fathers as they have cabins. There are not ten Fathers out of a hundred who could go through what we would have to endure, were we to follow them. We should have much work to do, and very little good would result from it, until we can succeed in making this tribe remain in one place. We cannot make them till the ground, for they know nothing about husbandry. Besides, where could their crops be lodged? Only in their cabins built of bark, where the very first frost would destroy them. They are a race who live from hand to mouth. Our only plan would be, sending amongst them men who were thoroughly conversant with the manner of bringing the ground under cultivation. If such men lived

---

(1) Relations of 1634, p, 12

amongst them, tilling the ground, perhaps the Montagnais Indians might settle down. This is a matter requiring great consideration. When men have always lived in idleness how can we habituate them to the rude labors attendant on cultivating the ground? We can get on easily enough with the Indians of the interior, such as the Hurons and the Algonquins, for they are stationary and grouped in regular villages, but, as for the Tadousac Indians, our chances of success with them would be very slight".

Four years after **the retaking of Quebec** from the Kertks the **Jesuits had** already **twenty-six representatives of their Order and six residences in the new colony. As early as 1626,** one of their member **had gone 300 leagues from** Quebec, to the **very centre** of the continent, **in** order to evangelize the Hurons. In 1636, Fathers Brebœuf, **Mercier,** Pijart, Chastellain, Garnier, **Jogues were** exercising their apostolate in that already **flourishing** mission. At Three Rivers, Fathers **Buteux and du Marché** were taking charge **of** the Algonquins and the

White Fish (Poissons Blancs). Quebec had two regular Jesuit establishments: Our Lady of Angels (Notre-Dame des Anges) and our Lady of Help (Notre-Dame de Recouvrance). Quebec was the head-quarters of the reserve army of Jesuits and it was there that the young recruits were formed for mission work. There was a Jesuit residence on the foggy island of Miscou near Bay des Chaleurs, as likewise on Cape Breton Island. The success achieved by the disciples of Loyola in Paraguay had inspired the Canadian Jesuits with the idea of founding establishments in New France similar to those in the former country. It had been a comparatively easy task organizing the Huron nation, for they already possessed some sort of a government, but it was a far more difficult task establishing order among the nomadic tribes whose hunting-grounds embraced the shores of the Lower St Lawrence. A good gentleman, whose zeal, had been stirred up by the perusal of the Relations, came most opportunely to the succor of the good Fathers and Sillery was founded. This village was built as an outpost of the budding colony of Quebec, and it was here that the Jesuits tried to collect their wandering flock. Those first gathered in enlisted others in the cause. A famous Tadousac captain or chief, having been converted, established himself at Sillery, and although his subjects, who of all the Indians were the least inclined to become Christians, absolutely refused to follow their chief to his new quarters, they ended by asking to have a missionary sent to them. If the mountain will not come to Mahomet, Mahomet must go to the mountain, says a proverb that dates from long ago. Since the Tadousac Indians would not leave their country, the Jesuits went there to them. In the month of May, 1641, Father Paul le Jeune, Father de Quen and Marsollet the interpreter, embarked for Tadousac (1). This was the commencement of the Jesuits' missionary work in that region and for nearly one hundred and fifty years, from 1641 to 1782, they unceasingly exercised the most arduous apostolate.

---

(1) Relations of 1641 p. 50; Relations of 1652.

"This is such a miserable country, wrote Father de Quen, that there is hardly sufficient earth for the purposes of sepulture. It is all barren, bare rock. However, it would do good to every one if the company, whose fleet spends some months here every year, would build a house, as Mons de Plessis-Bochart had commenced doing. Then the Fathers could come here every spring and remain till the vessels departed. I would not advise the French to remain there during the winter. The Indians go away during that season, leaving their rocks to the cold, the snow and the ice".

It was to this poor and desolate land that Father de Quen came year after year for more than 11 years (1) so that by cultivating it during the summer it might bear fruit in the winter (2). So soon as the river was free from ice, the Indians came to Quebec to fetch him in their canoes. They constructed a retired ca-

---

(1) 1631-1652.

(2) Relations of 1644.

bin for him which served as his dwelling and also as a chapel. It was there that he said his mass every day, thus sowing the good seed among the scattered nations of the Saguenay who frequented that port on account of the trading.

In order that his new vine might bear more abundant fruit, the Father much wished to build himself a house at Tadousac (1). His wish was accomplished. Following the example of Gamache and Sillery and of many great French ladies who had aided the missionaries by bestowing large gifts of money, the Duchess of Aiguillon in 1648, gave him wherewithal to maintain his mission. In that year, for the first time, he could say his mass in a small hut which had been hastily constructed by the French who were unloading the vessels.

That same year brick was brought from France in order to build the house at Tadousac (1). The following year, when Madame

) Relations of 1642.

(1) Relations

de la Pelterie came there from Quebec, she was godmother to two little Indians in this improvised chapel. Two Ursuline nuns who had arrived from France with Father le Jeune happened to be there at the same time and they all offered fervent thanksgiving to God. Never had the Saguenay nomads seen such a spectacle. Still greater was their astonishment when, in 1647, the chapel was embellished by some little drugget hangings and was endowed with a bell to call them to the services. The hangings were of a wavy pattern and the more superstitious among the Indians did not fail to suspect that some spell or sorcery was attached to them. As for the bell all of them took the greatest delight in listening to its sound. They themselves hung it as skilfully as a French artisan could have done. Each of them wanted to ring it himself, to see if would speak as well for him as for the Father.

From 1641, the Jesuits had never missed sending one or two of their Fathers to Tadousac every year to pass the summer there, aiding the French who landed at that port and working for the salvation of the Indians who flocked there. "At the approach of the winter, wrote an annalist of the order, when the country puts off its green vestment in order to assume a white robe and when the little crystals begin to form on the edges of the rivers and streams, the Indians separate in every direction and go in search of the elk, the deer, the caribou, the bear and the beaver. Each goes in his own direction, but only in the one agreed upon before separating from the others, so as not to interfere with each other in their hunting excursions. The Fathers then all returned to Quebec". Before their departure the missionaries selected "chiefs of prayer" from among the better instructed of the Indians and these chiefs were charged with recalling to the minds of their brethren, the notions of religion which had been imparted to them during the summer. Calendars were entrusted to these Dogiques so that they might know when the Sundays and feast-days fell, so as to keep them holy. It was they who were to decide any difficulties that might arise, to dictate what prayers were to be recited during illness, in time of trial, or when the chase was not productive, or again when rivers and lakes were to be crossed. These improvised chiefs of prayers had sometimes more zeal than common sense, like all newly-converted people.

"One day, records the annalist of the mission, Sieur de Joinville, who has written the life of St Louis, being overtaken at sea by a great tempest, his soldiers and sailors who thought themselves in danger of perishing, threw themselves at his feet and asked him to give them absolution of their sins. But, said he, do you think, I have the necessary powers? Who else can have them since there is no priest on board? On receiving this reply, he raised his voice: Well then, I absolve you with all the powers I possess, I do not know whether I have any, but if I have you are absolved. By acting thus he showed extraordinary simplicity, not unmixed with great ignorance. The Tadousac Indians in this first winter fell into similar error. Finding themselves in the depths of the woods, far away from a missionary, they **were** suddenly taken with a longing to hear mass. One of them went through the ceremonies with all the excess of fervor suggested. An old woman heard confessions. As to those who had committed some great fault, they had to confess the same publicly and be pitilessly scourged". One can well imagine the missionary's surprise when, on his return the following spring, he heard the account of these good people's religious performances.

It was Father de Quen, as we have already said, who was the most frequently sent on the Tadousac mission. His name is constantly being met with from 1641 to 1652. During this decade his occasional **fellow missioners were** Fathers Buteux, **Druillettes, Lyonne, Bailloquet.**

From the time of his first sojourn at Tadousac in 1641, Father de Quen had ardently desired to penetrate into the depths of the Saguenay district and visit the Indians of the northern tribes; but he had always been prevented doing so, through their apprehension of the secrets of their hunting grounds being betrayed. It was only in July 1647, that he could start on a journey to the Porcupine (Porc-Epic) **tribe**. He ascended the Saguenay and the rapids of the River Chicoutimi, traversed the great Kenogami lake and was the first Frenchman whose adventurous bark ploughed the waters of Lake St John. In 1652 he again made the **journey**. It was Father de Quen likewise who commenced the Betsiamites mission.

Father Charles Albanel became the regular successor of Father de Quen in the Tadousac Montagnais mission. He was the first missionary who commenced to follow the Indians in their winter hunting campaigns (1). From 1650 to 1660 he dwelt in these parts, sometimes going along the borders of the river, sometimes plunging into the woods, sometimes taking up his abode at Tadousac itself with the

(1) Journal of the Jesuits, p. 144.

few French whom the private companies had retained in their employ for the winter to look after their interests. During the winter of 1657 he ventured with a hunting-party on the south shore of the river and reached the Notre-Dame mountains. In the spring of 1660, before leaving Tadousac, Father Albanel had married a Frenchman named François Pelletier to an Indian Christian woman without publishing any banns or notifying the parents, the bishop, or the governor. This affair made a great sensation, and the Father was sent away to the Ottawa mission.

Serving the Tadousac mission had been a labor of love to Father Albanel; for ten years of his life he had bestowed all his care on it, and for its sake had made many a sacrifice. Yet, obedient to the rule of his Order, he left it promptly and hastened to other and unknown shores. St Ignatius says: " A Jesuit must resemble a soldier under marching orders." Father Albanel returned to Tadousac after ten years' absence; but, alas! he found everything changed. The church he had so long governed, the mission he had left so flourishing, now were but shadows of their former selves. Famine, sickness and an implacable enemy had dispersed the 1200 catechumens whom he had delighted to instruct. Solitude reigned once more on the rocks of Tadousac, and the Father found barely one hundred wan-looking Indians to greet his return.

Great events had happened since the day when Father Albanel had for the first time abandoned the shores of Tadousac. In 1660 immediately after his departure, Fathers Druillettes and Frémin (1) had been sent to replace him. The traders looked on them with an evil eye and in an underhand way had done all they could to hinder them from coming. The Fathers therefore had to retrace their steps almost immediately. The following year, the implacable Iroquois landed at Tadousac, surprised the French who were occupied with their fishing and unexpectant of evil, killed three of their

---

(1) Journal of the Jesuits, p. 285

number and dealt out destruction with both fire and sword. They spared nothing. The post-house or factory was destroyed, the church burned, the survivors of the inhabitants numbering about one hundred souls embarked for Quebec, Tadousac was left in ruins (2). It was after this audacious attack and on their way back to their **own** country that the Iroquois killed the High Seneschal, Jean de Lauzon, on the Island of Orleans.

For nearly two years after this disaster, Tadousac remained uninhabited, until, in the spring of 1663, Father Druillettes was again sent there. The Indians, who were kept away from the river shore by fear of the enemy, had **dispersed into** the depths of the woods or had sought refuge with tribes who resided further from the Gulf. In the course of his adventurous journeys, Father Bailloquet had penetrated into the country of the Papinachois, **a nation** situated to the north of Tadousac. This was in the year 1664. The Jesuits chose the latter

---

(2) Journal of the Jesuits, p. 296.

place as their place of refuge and it was thence that the missionaries started out in search of their scattered flocks. Fathers Druillettes, Bailloquet and Henri Nouvel succeeded each other there until 1668. We hear of them on the right side of the river, at Lake St John, at the Betsiamites, at the mission of Lake Barnaby in the Papinachois country. These missions were under the care of the Jesuit Father Louis de Beaulieu when Bishop de Laval landed at Tadousac in 1668 to give confirmation to the few Indians who still dwelt there or whom peace had again attracted to the spot. The temple that had cost such pains to construct having been reduced to ashes, the Bishop had to be received in a bark chapel (1).

Albanel had passed the winter of 1669 in the forest bordering Rivière-du-Loup, Notre-Dame du Portage and Green Island (Ile-Verte) and, in the spring of 1670, he was preparing to return to Quebec when he received orders to go to Tadousac and administer the last sacra-

---

(1) Relation of 1668.

ments to the sick, as also to bury the victims of an epidemic that was raging there. As he was proceeding along the north coast in a canoe in search of his dispersed flock, he met with an Indian from the celebrated North Bay * (Baie du Nord) who told him he had himself seen a French vessel in his own country.

Albanel questioned him closely, desiring nothing so much as to advance into their unexplored country.

For a long time the missionaries and governors of New France had been anxious to penetrate these mysterious forests and reach the famous sea. The English had the same desire, and which nation was the first to take possession is still a debated point, with no possibility of any decision being come to (1). On June 24th, 1640, an Englishman arrived in Quebec with twenty Abenaquis. He had left Kenebec, crossed the Alleghanies and descend-

---

* Hudson's Bay.

(1) See a very interesting study on this point by Mons Paul de Cazes : *The Northern Frontier (La Frontière Nord)*

sd the Chaudière as far as the St Lawrence in search of a passage to the North Sea. Mons. de Montmagny sent him to Tadousac, whence they shipped him to England. He replied to the Jesuits who questioned him, that by going up the Saguenay he was sure of reaching the sea. But the Fathers then thought the Lake Huron route was the more certain (1). In 1657, the Procureur General Jean Bourdon, in 1661 the missionary Fathers Dablon and Druillettes, in 1663, the notary Pierre Duquet, had vainly attempted the journey. Meanwhile the Indians had been incessantly interrogated, and every missionary had communicated whatever information he had gathered. The Relation of 1658 gives the details of six different routes which would finally lead to this mysterious sea, " routes that were far more difficult to follow than the high-road from Paris to Orleans ".

The solution of this problem was of the highest importance. If the English were once allowed to establish themselves on the foggy

---

(1) Relation 1640, p. 36.

shores of the Bay there was no hope of securing the trading with the northern nations who supplied the factories or trading posts of Three Rivers and Tadousac. What his predecessors had failed to do, Father Albanel accomplished.

Ten years previously, June 1st 1661, the missionary Dablon and Sieur de la Vallière had set out from Tadousac and mounting the Saguenay, Lake St John and the Assamachouanne, had arrived at Lake Nikouba on the highest grounds (1), a hundred leagues from the river and half way to North Bay (Baie du Nord). Father Albanel took a westerly direction. Having set out from Tadousac, August 8th 1671, he penetrated as far as Lake St John where he wintered. June 1st, 1672, he left his winter-quarters and, by the way of Rivière-aux-Sables and a succession of ponds or little lakes not yet named, arrived at the great Mistassini Lake on the eighteenth day. On the 25th of the month, he at length came to the celebrated northern sea. By the end of July he was

---

(1) Relation of 1661, Journal des Jésuites, p. 300.

again at Tadousac where the Frenchmen of the trading-post helped him to celebrated the anniversary of his departure. Father Albanel had traversed 800 leagues on foot and in canoes, had passed 200 waterfulls and 100 rapids, and all in the space of less than sixty days (1). Until then, says the Relation, this journey had been supposed to be impossible for the French who had already undertaken it three times and unable to overcome the obstacles they met with had found themselves obliged to abandon the entreprise, despairing of success ". To Father Albanel belongs the glory of having accomplished the expedition that had occupied his thoughts for eighteen years.

Father Albanel's journey terminates the era of discovery in the regions to the north of Tadousac. It is now a country that is well known, even though not thoroughly explored, and we shall now see the Jesuits, still keeping Tadousac as their rallying-point, extending a

---

(1) This would appear impossible, but see Relation of 1672, p. 48.

net-work of establishments and temporary missions over the country whose dark veil they had torn asunder. We shall see the traders, eager for booty, following the intrepid missionaries, and the factory or trading building rearing its head side by side with the rustic chapel.

Father Albanel's successor, Father François de Crépieul, during his thirty-one years' apostolate, from 1671 to 1702, had to serve the whole of this vast region. Setting out from Ste Croix of Tadousac, and going to the North, he would come to the missions of St Francis-Xavier of Chicoutimi and St Charles of Metabetchouan, to the extreme East he would arrive at the sources of the Assamachouanne and at the establishment of St Ignatius of Nikouba, to the West he would find the the post of the Holy Family, in the centre of Mistassini Lake. Returning to his starting-point and going along the north shore of the river he would come successively to Our Lady of Good Desire (Notre-Dame du Bon-Désir) of the Bergeronnes, to L'Escoumain, to Betsiamites, to Our Lady of the Assumption of the Jeremiah Islands (îlets

Jérémie) to the mission of The Guardian Angel among the Oumamiois, to that of the Lake St Barnaby at the head of the River Ste Marguerite.

Eight assistants came successively to the aid of the missionary. They were Fathers Jean-Baptiste Boucher, Jean Morain, Antoine Silvy, Bonaventure Fabre, Antoine Dalmas, Louis André, Pierre Marest, Jean Chardon. Silvy, Dalmas and Marest went as far as Hudson's Bay. Father Marest was made prisoner by the English and taken to Plymouth, Father Dalmas was killed by the Indians of Fort Ste Anne. This was the only martyr whom the Jesuits gave to the missions in the North.

After the departure of the Father François de Crépieul, the missions of those distant regions appear to have been somewhat abandoned. The Jesuit Father Laure, who seems to have been his first regular successor, declares in his Journal that on arriving at Chicoutimi, he is taking possession of the missions which have been newly established after an interregnum of twenty years. Father Laure died at the Eboulements in 1738 and was replaced two years afterwards by Father Jean-Baptiste Maurice. Father Maurice died at Tadousac, March 20th, 1746, and in the autumn of that same year, Father Claude-Godfroi Coquart received orders to go there and continue his predecessor's work. Father Coquart, in his turn, died July 4th, 1765, and the missionary who interred him at Chicoutimi, Father Jean-Baptiste de la Brosse, was the twenty-first missionary of his order in that region.

Chicoutimi, under the reign of Fathers Laure and Coquart, appears to have taken the lead of Tadousac. "The Jesuits are now in possession of this mission which is at Chicoutimi", says la Potherie (1). Charlevoix complains of the solitude of Tadousac where there were neither men nor beasts to be seen (2).

During one hundred and forty-two years, the missions of Tadousac and the Saguenay

---

(1) p. 208.

(2) (1721).

were under the apostolic care of the disciples of St Ignatius of Loyola, and, during that century and a half, the history of Tadousac contains little else than a record of the works which these Fathers performed. Since the year 1783 secular priests have replaced the Jesuits.

VII

Explorations of the Jesuit missionaries.—Their diplomacy.—How they became valuable auxiliaries to the government.

The work of the Jesuit missionaries was not confined to evangelizing the Indians, but was of a twofold nature. Apostles and soldiers, the Jesuits penetrated everywhere, seeking out the most obscure haunts in order there to lay down their lives in the name of God and of the King of France. To the same extent they relied on the State, the State relied on them. As missionaries, they worked for the conversion of the tribes, as political agents they watched their converts closely, keeping them away from the English and imparting the results of their observations. They did not live for themselves, they lived for their religion and their country. Every Indian whom they converted became an ally of France. All the Indian tribes, from Acadia to Mississippi, have been under their two-fold influence. When the glory of the French name was at stake, the missionary, the warrior and the trader acted in unison. It would seem as if this alliance cemented by their having shared such numerous perilous missions reposed on too solid a basis to be easily severed. Nevertheless, as soon as the common enemy had disappeared, these heroes who had previously been so united, indulged in discussions worthy of a less civilized age, and by these discussions often destroyed the fruits of many a victory they had together gained at the cost of great sacrifices.

To the Indian chief who wished to close the road to the North Sea, Father Albanel replied : " It is not for the sake of purchasing a passage across this river and your lake that I wished to make you two presents. Since the French have delivered your country from the incursions of your enemies, the Iroquois, they well deserve full liberty to go and come across this land which they have acquired by their arms. Besides, God, whom you yourselves say is the master of all since it is He who has created everything and who governs everything, by sending me to make His name known throughout all lands, confers on me the right to pass freely everywhere I may wish.... I love God, the Frenchman says to you, and I wish for no allies, no family, who take the demon for their master, and have recourse to him in their needs. My friendship, my alliance and my relationship must not be only earthly and of this world, but must continue after death and have their fruition in Heaven. Therefore, abandon your design of trading with the Europeans who carry on their trade in the region of the North Sea, where they do not pray to God; direct your steps once more towards Lake St John, where you will always find some *black robe* to instruct and baptize you (1).

It was thus in the year of grace, 1671, in the depths of the Saguenay woods, Father Albanel cemented the union of Church and State, advocating the interests of the two in one and the same harangue.

---

(1) Relation of 1672, p. 48.

Among the Huron and Iroquois tribes, the Jesuits had many glorious missions which they baptized with their blood—missions worthy of apostles and martyrs. The church of Tadousac was more humble. Though she has never been tried by fire and sword, history records that protracted journeyings and prodigious labors were accomplished by the Jesuits who were the discoverers and pioneers of these regions. They were the first to penetrate into those distant solitudes so replete with mystery and of which so many awe-inspiring legends were related. The Saguenay and the regions to the north were they better known than they are at the present day? It must not be forgotten that, in those primitive times when a road to Japan was being so ardently sought for, it was at Tadousac that the expeditions of 1671 and 1681 were organized and it was thence that the discovering parties set forth in search of the celebrated North Sea, which they eventually reached. It is to the labors of the Jesuits that we are indebted for our knowledge of those regions, and their labors have been related by the Fathers with an amount of humility that could only be equalled by their devotedness.

When the capital of New France was barely emerging from its extreme infancy, the Jesuits already had missions established along the Saguenay and on the shores of Lake St John. At the end of the last century when Michaux, the naturalist, was advancing northwards, by the way of Mistassini and Rupert, he was following in the traces of Father Albanel. The Jesuit Father Laure, who lived at Tadousac from 1720 to 1737, has left a map of the Saguenay territory which is still a marvel to geographers through the abundance and rigorous exactness of its details. In Charlevoix's book, we are surprised to find a map of these countries in which Lake Mistassini is marked with all its bays and its numerous little islands, all of which latter bear completely French names such as: St Joseph's, Holy Cross, St Ambroise, St John (îles Saint Joseph, Sainte-Croix, Saint-Ambroise, Saint-Jean). On a peninsula separating Lakes Albanel and Dauphin from Lake Mistassini, the house of Dorval is marked. The rivers Bourbon, Red Carp (à la Carpe Rouge), and Pêche Nouvelle discharge themselves into this inland sea.

In 1702, the missionary Father Crépieul tells us that one Nicolas went to the Grand Lake Mistassini accompanied by ten Frenchmen and two Montagnais Indians in order to rebuild his house and reconstruct the general cemetery and the infants' cemetery. From the time of Father Albanel's journey the Jesuits had a mission on Lake Mistassini which they served regularly and even they had founded an establishment on Lake Nikouba after Father Dablon's expedition in 1661.

And now, at the end of this nineteenth century, these regions are again unknown! A surveyor who had gone up nearly to the source of the old des Sables river whence he believed he could perceive Lake Mistassini has related his exploits, and, in certain quarters, this simple fact has been spoken of as a glorious discovery.

It was by means of these very maps that the surveyors found their way to the unknown region, when in 1828 the Canadian government sent an exploring party to examine the Lake St John valley, an old trapper having revealed its existence and spoken of its marvels to the astonished deputies. It was the Relations of these pioneers that furnished those gentlemen with most of their information.

The primitive Indians, fearing that their hunting-grounds might be appropriated, had represented to the missionaries that the interior of the Saguenay country was barren and mountainous, covered with perpetual snow and of a most unpleasant aspect. An echo of these first accounts of the district may be found in Champlain and in some of the writers who succeeded him. The trading companies, like the Indians, had no desire to encourage the establishment or invite the competition of any newcomers in the haunts they frequented for the fur-trade and they had always sought to prevent too much being known by strangers about these countries.

The Jesuits, who had none of these notions, tell us, in the Relations, all they had seen, concealing neither the fertility of the land, nor the mildness of the climate. Their accounts of their travels, printed and spread both in France and in the colony (1), were splendid guides to the future colonists in search of suitable places to settle. The Conquest interfered with their work of preparation. In the first instance, it had been necessary to people the valley of the St Lawrence, and then the government having founded the military establishments on the Richelieu had concentrated its energies in the direction of the Great Lakes and the Mississippi where it was of great consequence that officially organized groupings should connect the colony of Louisiana. When Quebec fell, the valley of La Beauce had only been cleared about twenty

---

(1) During the occupation of the country by the French, many Canadian families possessed copies of the Relations of the Jesuits, as may be seen by referring to the inventories of their possessions.

years. Besides, it was found necessary to advance towards the south and the west in order to resist the encroachments of the Anglo-Saxon race. The north had been reserved to us from all eternity. To meet the necessities of the times, the advanced posts of the Mistassini and Nikouba would amply suffice as rallying points for the Indians who were tempted to trade with the English vessels continually arriving in Hudson's Bay.

However this may be, let us hear how Father Dablon speaks of Lake St John : " This lake has a fine aspect, he writes in 1661, with a few scattered islands towards its mouth ; after which it gently rolls its waters over a fine sand, bounding it all round, the shape of the lake being somewhat oval ; it is about seven or eight leagues in diameter. It seems as if crowned by a beautiful forest, which shadows its shores, and, from whichever side we look at it, we behold a verdant expanse like a natural amphitheatre of twenty miles in circumference. It is not very deep considering the great number of rivers which flow into it, and which must increase its volume since it discharges itself by only one outlet, the River Saguenay, of which it is the source ". " This is a beautiful spot, the land is level and appears to be good, there being some fine meadow-land ; the otter the Canadian elk, the beaver and more especially the porcupine are here found in large numbers", writes Albanel, ten years later. This last missionary speaks as follows of Mistassini, Nemiskau and the slope towards the North Sea : " This country is not mountainous, the climate is milder than elsewhere, the land is good and very productive, so that it could support a large population if it were properly brought under cultivation. There are vast plains agreeably interspersed with water.... A great mistake has been made by those who represent this country as uninhabitable, either on account of the excessive cold, of the snow and ice, or of the scarcity of wood for building purposes or for fuel. They cannot have seen the vast thick forests, the beautiful plains and far-stretching meadows which border the rivers in various places and which are covered with all kinds of pasture. On the 15th of June I have myself seen wild-roses as beautiful and fragrant as any to be found at Quebec, the season appearing to me to be forwarder than there, whilst the air is mild and pleasant. There was no night when I was there, the evening twilight lasting until the early dawn".

These hardy explorers, these wonderful instruments in the hands of Divine Providence for the spread of civilization and of their own language, had been formed in a severe school. Many of them had abandoned their college chairs and their professorships of literature and the abstruse sciences, in order to plunge into the deepest recesses of the forests and become the humblest of teachers. When they passed through any country, they made a study of all its resources. It was Lafitau who discovered the ginseng. It was Charles Lemoine, whilst on a mission to the Iroquois, who first made known the famous salt-springs of Onondaga which the

Indians believed to be haunted by a wicked spirit. The mines of Lake Superior were also described by the Jesuits. They gathered simples or medicinal herbs, catalogued them and made drawings of them. Father de Beaulieu, one of the most learned mathematicians of his time, a missionary at Tadousac, after having hunted and shot all day, would amuse himself in the evenings by dissecting the game in order to become acquainted with its anatomy; his only luminary being the torch's smoky glare.

" The Hurons and other sedentary tribes are, as it were, the aristocracy of the country, says Sagard. The Algonquin tribes compose the middle class, whilst the lowest class is represented by the Montagnais ". The art of tilling the ground had to be shewn to these nomadic tribes by means of example and these holy missionaries had themselves to undertake the manual labor of clearing the land and bringing it into cultivation.

These evangelical pioneers founded their agricultural establishment on the borders of

Lake St John, at the mouth of the River Metabetchouan. From the primeval forest they took three hundred acres, which they converted into a superb farm, where cereals grew as well as in the fertile valley of the St Lawrence. In 1828, **the** exploring party sent by the Canadian government discovered on the above-mentioned spot the traces of furrows which had been made by the ploughs **of** the missionaries in the land they had cleared. They were hidden under the spruce-trees, aspens, fir-trees and birches which had grown them, but grass still grew there **in** abundance. The orchards, which some old trappers well remembered having seen there, had disappeared. Only two plum-trees and a few gooseberry-brushes remainded as vestiges of former cultivation.

To supply this distant farm with requisites, the Jesuits **had** found means of opening a road betwen Quebec and Lake St John, and **it** was along this road **that** they sent **up** their cattle to market. It is said that it took only three days to accomplish the journey between the two places. The existence of this rough road across the forest, along the mountain gorges and through the valleys has been doubted by many authorities, but tradition speaks so positively of it that it is difficult not to believe the road existed. Those who distrust these legendary tales are referred to the indications of this road marked on the map engraved by Bellin in 1744. On this map, which is inserted at the 64th page of Charlevoix, third volume, a road is marked between two chains of mountains, which road led to Lake St Charles behind Quebec and commenced on the Saguenay near Anse St Jean (1) (St John's Creek).

(1) Until 1842 the first colonists of the Saguenay valley had no other communication by land with the Charlevoix parishes than by means of a path leading from Anse St Jean to Malbaie (Murray Bay). But in the course of that year, some Indians having pointed out that a road could easily be opened between Baie St Paul and la Grande Baie, the route was explored and, the statement of the Indians being verified, a road was marked out.

We have nowhere been able to find by what right the Jesuits held their landed property at Metabetchouan. Doubtless, this domain was held under the grant made by the king to the Company of Jesus, of a league of ground wherever there existed a fort or a royal establishment.

It is not known when the Jesuits abandoned their Lake St John settlement, but, for more than three quarters of a century, the regular presence of representatives of the Order is proved by the registers of Chicoutimi and Tadousac. From 1691 to 1699, for example, Father Bonaventure Fabre styles himself "Missionary of St Charles of Metabetchouan of the Lake St John which falls into the Chicoutimi river".

As early as 1656 (1) the Governor Jean de Lauzon, in the name of the Company of New France, had given to the Jesuits a piece of land at Tadousac, as a freehold, which land they were to select wherever they found it most suitable for building a church and a priest's residence and for making a cemetery. This gift was confirmed by the king, May 12th, 1678. On this piece of land which consisted of six square arpents (2), the missionaries built the

---

(1) July 1st.

(2) Report of the commission named in 1787.

An *arpent* is an old French land measure and is equivalent to a little less than 2 acres: *3 roods*.

edifices necessary for worship and commenced an agricultural establishment of which the vestiges still exist and which is known in the country by the name of *the Jesuit's garden* (*Jardin des Jésuites*). The old inhabitants still tell wonders of the orchard and the fruit-trees which grew there up to some fifty years ago.

It is a fact worthy of remark that wherever the Jesuits dwelt, even temporarily, in this region, they attempted some sort of cultivation beside the rustic temple and the humble presbytery.

The rugged chain of the Laurentides runs along the north shore of the Lower St Lawrence from the extremity of the Labrador peninsula as far as about ten leagues below Quebec where it abruptly turns inland. For an unbroken course of more than a hundred leagues, the peaks of these mountains hide their haughty heads in the clouds and their rocky sides, incessantly battered by the waves, present an inaccessible face to the storm-tossed mariner.

The slopes of these rocks that are towards the sea have, here and there, narrow defiles in which the cod or herring fisher can dry his nets. The north slope of the Laurentian mountains opens on to an excessively wild country interspersed with rivers which long remain ice-bound. This vast empire out of which twenty provinces could be made has but scant herbage and a few dwarfed trees hardly producing wherewithal to feed some few flat-faced Esquimaux families.

It was in these sea-girt regions, barren and shadeless, that the Indians from the interior formerly pitched their tents during the summer, and it was here that the missionaries from Tadousac came to meet them.

The missionaries, in trying to create an agricultural establishment in the Lake St John valley, did a very meritorious work. They wanted to gather together the scattered remains of the nomadic tribes, and lead them away from where they found but a meagre subsistence. They strove to habituate them to a more stationary life on lovely lands amidst forests teeming with all sorts of game, where twenty large tribes had formerly dwelt at ease. For a long time, then, the post of Tadousac was deserted. The greater part of the Montagnais tribe had abandoned it in order to group themselves around the establishments in the interior.

We have here given a rough sketch of a part of what the Jesuits undertook in the ancient kingdom of the Saguenay. Truly was it an arduous task to be performed by a mere handful of men amidst the silence of the woods, and its accomplishment required the exercise of admirable self-abnegation and unbounded devotedness. Valuable auxiliaries to the State, they certainly did enough to have had a prominent place in the budget of the colony on account of the invaluable services they had rendered Alas! large remunerations were not to be bestowed on these hardy workers in the field. Apart from the piece of land given them by Lauzon in 1656, and the Metabetchouan domain which they cultivated with their own hands we have shewn that the Jesuits, for the support of a missionary at Tadousac, only received annually from the State the sum of six hundred *livres* (1), which represents in our money of the present time the enormous sum of one hundred dollars.

They have been accused of trading with the Indians. According to our belief, this accusation cannot be borne out as regards the missionaries in the Saguenay district; we ourselves certainly have found no traces of such traffic; they had to play a most painful part in this corner of the continent, and they performed their self-appointed task with the greatest disinterestedness, making the best of everything.

One of their number, François de Crépieul, has given us a very touching narrative of these missions. He did not write it out of vain-glory, but for the instruction and greater consolation of those who should come after him.

"The life of a Montagnais missionary, he says, is a long and cruel martyrdom, entailing

---

(1) Quebec collection of manuscripts, III-vol. p. 137.

nearly incessant mortification and trials of patience ; it is indeed a life of penance and humiliation particularly in the huts of the Indians and when travelling with them.

"The huts are made of birch-bark and poles, surrounded by branches of the fir-tree to cover the snow and frozen ground.

"The missionary spends nearly all the day seated or kneeling, exposed to perpetual smoke in the winter-time.

"He often perspires during the day and generally suffers from the cold during the night. He sleeps without undressing, on the frozen earth, sometimes on the snow with but a few branches of trees to cover him.

"He eats from a vessel which is seldom washed or cleaned, it being more frequently either wiped with a dirty piece of skin from some animal or licked by the dogs. He eats when there happens to be anything to eat and when something happens to be offered him. Sometimes the meat is but half cooked, sometimes it is very tough, especially the meat which has been smoked and dried in the chimney.

What repast there is, is cooked in a pot but once a day, or twice in times of plenty, but there is generally little enough of it".

. . . .

This is a true recital, sketched from life, for the information of the novices preparing to undertake this rough life.

Now let us see how cheerfully these men bore with these hardships of which they had full knowledge before going to encounter them. A missionary accompanying a hunting party in the neighborhood of Tadousac is now speaking : " Every place serves us as a hostelry, built in the snow, where neither bread, wine, salt, sauce, nor ragout is to be found, but only a very good appetite. The missionary lodges always in the same hostelry, finds always the same bed awaiting him, which bed has existed since the beginning of the world, and since Adam's days has never been shaken up except by some earthquake or other. A good appetite makes him find a bit of smoked meat, dry as leather, as delicate eating as a young partridge. Fatigue obtains for him sweet sleep. God keeps him in good health, and his legs and oars in conjunction with the oars of his boat-companions bring him to the end of his journey in time for him to undertake another one immediately ".

This same Crépieul, whose lamentable description of a missionary's life we have just heard, ends his account of his first winter passed at Tadousac by telling his superior : " The greatest favor I can ask of you is to grant me the same happiness next year, during which I hope that God may give me courage to repair by fresh sufferings the faults I have committed this year ".

Father Henri Nouvel, returning from a mission among the Papinachois, one of the most difficult of the north coast, intones a song of triumph : *Magnificat Domino mecum, et exaltemus nomen ejus in idipsum* (1).

All these missionaries of the Tadousac region have left journals of their travels. The Relations of the Jesuits printed at Quebec contain some twenty of them, from 1641 to

---

(1) Relation of 1664.

1672. The same courageous tone is to be found in all of them.

Certainly most wonderful strength was necessary to enable these men to continue such gigantic efforts for several years, but the Jesuits knew admirably well how to inspirit the members of their Order.

Those destined for the missions commenced their preparation long previously to their departure for the scene of their labors. They had to consider beforehand what amount of work and hardship they would have to encounter, and when once their sacrifice was made and their resolution taken, nothing could make them quail or go back from what they had undertaken. They had been formed to their task by a rigorous discipline and that discipline kept them on the alert. The instructions which Father le Jeune had prepared for the use of the missionaries of his order are well worth perusing. They will give us the best insight into the source of the vigor displayed by these athletes, and will make us understand how they acquired such influence over the nations to whom they were sent.

"Reckon up beforehand all the labors, the hardships, the perils which must be encountered during your journeyings, writes Father le Jeune(1), so that you may be prepared for whatever may happen. Love the Indians well! Never let yourself be waited for when you are to embark in a canoe. Provide yourself with a gun and with a burning mirror so as to be able to strike a light for your companions on the road, in day time, to light their pipes, at night time when preparing their cabins. Such little services as these will win their hearts.

"Force yourselves to eat *sagamite*, however dirty or insipid it may be. Bear with every thing. Refuse nothing which they offer you, for fear of displeasing them. Force yourselves to eat at daybreak. You must be quick in embarking and disembarking. Tuck up your habits so as not to carry any water or sand

---

(1) Relations of 1637.

into the canoes. Go bare-foot and bare-legged. Do not speak too much during your journeys. Do not question them too much about their language. You will learn nothing, and it bothers them. Silence is a useful possession at those times. Try to be always joyous. Each one of you will be furnished with half a gross of awls, two or three dozen of small knives, a hundred or so of fish-hooks and some drinking cups so as to feast the Indians. Strive to carry something at the portages (carrying-places). However little you carry, even should it be only a pot, the Indians are pleased that you should do it. Do not be ceremonious with them. Take care that your hats do not interfere with any one in the canoes. It would be better to wear your night caps. Do not begin by rowing, unless you intend rowing all the time. When in their own country, the Indians will retain the same opinion of you as they have formed on the journey. If you have passed for being tiresome and difficult to please, you will have much trouble in changing their opinion of you. It is perfectly incredible how they remember and remark the slightest fault or error. Give every one a good reception. They care **nothing** about your philosophy and theology. **If you can go** naked and carry a horse's load, as they **do,** you will be looked on by them as a great and learned man ".

It was thus **that the** Jesuits formed their missionaries. Can **any** such subtly minute and cleverly combined instructions be found emana**ting from any** diplomatic bureau whatever ?

VIII

Of the primitive Saguenay churches.—The Tadousac chapel.

Although the Jesuits looked upon the north-shore missions as *moveable churches*, we have seen what pains they expended on arresting the wanderings of the Indian tribes and changing their nomadic habits into more settled ones. After having long followed them in their hunting excursions through the forest, where the Fathers said Mass, sometimes on a felled tree (1), sometimes on the side of a canoe, the sails often serving as a canopy, they began here and there to lay the foundations of rustic churches near the more frequented trading-posts. At first these were but long cabins of bark or foliage, much like those which the Indians of Tadousac had put up in 1642 when Father de Quen arrived. The traders of this

---

(1) **Relation** of 1665

post had afterwards reserved a room in their factory where the Blessed Sacrament could be installed. We have already seen with what joy the artless children of the forest had received the drugget hangings and the bell which had been sent from France in 1647. In 1556, the Company of the One Hundred Associates gave the Jesuits a piece of land at Tadousac on which to construct a church and a residence. An entry in the Journal kept by the Fathers at Quebec tells us that in 1659 the projected erections were about completed. " November 21st, writes the annalist (1), Father Albanel set out to winter at Tadousac with Guillaume Boivin and Mons. Pelletier on the one hand and two sailors on the other. It was an experiment we were making to see whether it would do to repeat it, since we had never before done anything of the sort ; Guillaume Boivin was at our cost, but not François Pelletier, although under our name". This first Tadousac church was

---

(1) p. 268

built of stone. Montreal had as yet only a church built of wood.

During the incursion made by the Iroquois on Tadousac shores in 1661, this first church appears to have been miraculously protected, but although it then escaped ruin it was destroyed four years afterwards by a calamitous conflagration, as Mère de l'Incarnation tells us (1). "It is a very great loss, she adds, because it was a retreat for the traders, and a refuge for the French and the Indians. For this reason there is no appearance of the one or the other being left to the incursions of the enemy. I think it will have to be built again next spring".

The pious desire of this holy recluse did not so soon meet with its fulfilment. In 1668, when Bishop Laval made his pastoral visit and stopped at Tadousac, the church had not yet been rebuilt and the Indians, to their great regret, were obliged to receive the Chief of Prayer in a bark cabin.

---

(1) Letter 71.

The farmers of the trading post, however, did not long delay raising the church from its ruins [1]. The church was a powerful help to them in grouping the Indians around their trading-factory.

Notes left by the missionaries tells us that in different places on the coast they had erected churches in which to assemble the natives. On arriving in the Gulf these churches were to be met with at the Jeremiah islands (ilets Jérémie) at Betsiamites and at Seven Islands (Sept-Iles). The missions of Lake St John and Mistassini had their residences, oratories and cemeteries.

In 1675, the Indians gave the missionaries elk, beaver and otter skins, as well as necklaces made of porcelain, in order that they might commence building a chapel at Lake St John.

The following summer, Pierre de Bécart, sieur de Grandville, went to the Lake and selected a piece of land, at the entrance of the

---

[1] In 1671.

Metabetchouan river, as the most advantageous spot for establishing a trading post. He had a chapel put up as well as a house, and it was here that the first cross was planted on these shores. "The annotator of the old register says : by his authority and his example he contributed to hurrying on the works during all the time that he stayed at that place. To replace him, he left Mons. de la Montagne who did not spare himself in any way and remained there till all was finished on September 12th. Charles Cadieu and Joseph du Buisson helped on the works very much during the ten or twelve days they were there".

As far back as 1671, the traders had built a house at Chicoutimi. In the summer that the establishment of St Charles de Metabetchouan was begun, Sieur de Grandville caused one Jean Langlois to build at Chicoutimi another chapel 30 feet long, with a room for the priest and a little sacristy. " He pointed out the place where it was to stand, June 24th, and helped it on by his efforts, good management and example, for he himself worked at it from time to time, and he did the same for the cemetery which was finished September 7th. Messieurs de Maure and la Vallée did not either spare themselves in any way".

Mons. Bazire to whom the grant had been made of the Saguenay trading-factories had been at the expense of all these erections. He also caused a church, which he had promised, to be built for the Papinachois, to which church Captain de Courville, of the bark *Ste Catherine*, also contributed largely by his exertions and his authority.

It was, in 1688, that, through the exertions of Father de Crépieul, a little house dedicated to St Nicholas was finished at Lake Mistassini. There was also a church there with considerable dependencies.

It would appear that, later on, the Jesuits reimbursed Mons. Bazire for the expense he had been put to in the construction of the Lake St John chapel, but the house was a gift bestowed personally by Mons. Aubert de la Chenaye.

For keeping up these missions scattered over an immense tract of country, for constructing and decorating these churches which were hidden away in the depths of the woods, the Jesuits had neither tithe nor fees, nor capitation money. The king had given them considerable landed property in various parts of the country, the revenues of which estates were to be employed either for the conversion of the heathen in general or for certain tribes in particular or to aid in the instruction of the children of the colony. These seigniories or landed estates, which are now estimated as being worth more than a million, were then but very little explored. The quit-rents paid by the copy-holders of these lands barely covered the first expenses and the annual disbursements necessary for the fulfilment of the obligations imposed on the lord of the manor (châtelain) by the feudal system.

We have already seen that the remuneration given by the metropolitan to the Tadousac missionary was so small that it hardly equalled the present pay of a beadle.

The good Fathers, however, found means to interest many an illustrious personage in their work, as also many a humbler member of the Church. Alms flowed into their hands from all directions. Each year, the Indians, the rich merchants of the colony, pious ladies, the farmers of the trading, gave largely to the missions.

The list of of the benefactors of the Saguenay churches is long. The Jesuits have preserved records of all that was given them. One can follow closely the offerings of all these pious souls during more than a century. They are recorded in the margins of the mission registers, in the dusty books and yellow leaves which still escape the ravages of time. Sometimes in Latin, sometimes in French, we read the acknowledgments of the gifts, the more modest of which are recorded as well as the more valuable ones. Not one is forgotten.

Who can find fault with these apostles for having patiently noted down daily the fact that a poor trapper had given a plane or a gimlet, an unknown Indian some bark? No detail is irksome when it concerns so distant an epoch.

The Quebec Seminary possesses in its archives the oldest register of these missions. It must have come into their possession when, at the commencement of this century, one of the directors of that institution went on the northern missions. It is preserved as a precious treasure. This register extends as far back as the year 1695, nearly to the foundation of the mission. The following one is missing and it is not known what has become of it. In the archives at Chicoutimi, however, is to be found a *résumé* that takes us to somewhere about the Conquest. At the Cardinal's palace the archivist has in charge the registers since 1759. Father Coquart who commenced this last series has inscribed on the first page the following touching appeal: " I pray all those who shall in future write in this book, of their charity to remember him who has commenced it, both in their holy sacrifices and their prayers".

The offerings came from various sources, as we have said. The Indians never failed to contribute a large share yearly. In 1646, the Tadousac Christians gave an alms of enough beaver-skins to buy in France four pieces of carpeting that must have cost 60 livres of French money. With these alms, the Fathers were also able to procure two large wooden candlesticks, two blank-books, one in which to register the baptisms, the other for registering the marriages and deaths. They also received four middle-sized pictures, a large cloth and the bell weighing 40 lbs which was hung in 1647.

These poor denizens of the woods gave the first fruits of their chase : beaver's fat, lean or black, otters, cariboo and elk skins, martens, spotted skins raw or dressed, goblets and necklaces of porcelain. The spotted skins made superb altar fronts and the missionaries were very proud of them.

One Indian would offer twenty beavers in satisfaction for some fault. Another would give a tent consisting of eight cariboo skins wherewith to cover the Papinachois church. In 1676, the Algonquin Indians from Three-Rivers gave a robe of six beaver-skins for the Lake St John chapel. Louis Mistagué one day offers two beavers and a dressed skin in order to repair the scandal he has caused by leaving his legitimate wife. Here is another one who lays two otter skins at the Father's feet in reparation of having cut down a cross on the river. This sort of penance was very efficacious.

Sometimes funeral offerings are the more numerous. A chief presents two robes to the Lake chapel, in remembrance of his two deceased brothers who were buried in the cemetery. A poor mother at her child's funeral would cover the coffin with presents. These offerings are very numerous. Widows would offer on the death of their husbands the guns of which the deceased had made use when hunting. At another time, a whole tribe would make some public offering to the church in order that an expedition might be fortunate. The Papinachois, wishing to have a bell and the *Lives of the Saints*, bring fox skins.

The missionaries remitted these presents to the farmers of the trading, who, in return furnished them with wood, nails, agricultural implements, carpenter's tools, church ornaments, or provisions. Monsieur Bazire, a great Quebec merchant, to whom for a long time the right of trading had been conceded, distinguished himself by his generosity. We have already seen him largely contributing to the erection of churches in the districts of Tadousac, Chicoutimi and St Charles of Lake St John. Among the signal benefactors, we find the names of Messieurs Juchereau de St Denis, de la Ferté, de la Chenaye, Riverin, de Grandville, de la Chevrotière, de Vilray, la Ville, a superior officer of the chancellery in France and director of the royal farm The names of the humble workmen who worked at the erection of these rustic chapels are entered with the same exactitude as those of the more distingushed donors.

Mademoiselle Bazire, for nearly twenty years, worked with her own hands at the church linen of the Saguenay sanctuaries. We would never end were we to mention all the pious women who generously followed her example.

The Ursuline and Hospital nuns of Quebec and Mme d'Ailleboust kept the linen in repair, made the flowers destined for the decoration of the sanctuaries, prepared delicacies for the sick and made clothing for the poor. Simular alms too arrived even from France. **The Augustinian and Benedictine nuns from Arras, the Ursulines from Amiens, the Ladies of Peace, sent boxes of beads, trinkets, statues, pictures and relics.** A touching incident **is recorded:** During more than fifteen years Father **de** Crépieul's mother and brothers annually sent **ten** crowns **to** the Saguenay mission.

The Jesuit Fathers **of** the Quebec **house** sent a great number of pictures and crucifixes to these churches. **We** have counted more than sixty pictures sent between 1678 and 1690, **without** speaking of representations where St Francis-Xavier and St Ignatius are the **principal** figures. Some of these pictures **are** on canvass, others on copper, with handsome gilt frames.

Each **church** had **its** bell for calling the

faithful to prayer, We see Mons. Dombourg, in 1687, giving the cabin-bell from his vessel for a new chapel. In the autumn of 1680, the vessel *l'Archange St Michel* went ashore and those on board gave the ship's bell to the northern missions. Similar gifts were made three or four times.

Certainly, with all these donations, there must have been considerable treasure in the Saguenay churches. We here give a list of what belonged to the chapel when Father F. Crépieul came to take charge of the Tadousac mission in 1671, an inventory having been made expressly :

An oil painting that could serve as an altar frontal, on which were depicted all the instruments of the Passion.

A complete set of altar-furniture in variegated silk, consisting of a higly-finished chasuble, an altar-frontal, veil, bourse, a humeral veil, a carpet, a large super-frontal, two large pieces of hangings with curtains and fringes. A piece of red linen to wrap up the above named, a pall. A censer, with its incense-boat and brass spoon. An altar-frontal of flowered stuff to match the drugget. A humeral veil of figured satin which hangs over the altar-picture of the crucifixion. Four pictures painted on copper with their frames. Two smaller pictures on wood. A wooden crucifix for processions and interments. Two brass candlesticks. Two large pieces of Bergamo tapestry. Two new window-blinds. A fine paper spotted with crosses which the Father sent to cover the altar. A surplice. A square cap. A large coffer (1).

In time these treasures increased, and the humble annalists of those days take a certain pleasure in yearly enumerating them, going into minutest details. First they mention the vestments, the chasubles, the stoles, the maniples, the flowered bourses ornamented with gold or silk braid, fine albs trimmed with lace, amices, fine linen communion-cloths, corporals, purificators, flowered humeral veils bordered with gold-braid, ciboriums, cruets, candle-sticks, tapers, copper holy-water founts. The walls of

---

(1) Oct. 29th, 1671, M. S. at Quebec Seminary.

the church are hung with Bergamo tapestry, red ratteen lace or splendid wild-beast skins.

To each chapel was attached a residence and a garden. These presbyteries were by no means princely, but it appears that they always contained a great collection of rude carpenter's tools and agricultural implements.

The mission of St Charles of Metabetchouan on Lake St John was the most favored. The annalist complacently gives us a list of all the tools deposited there, large and small planes of all sorts, chisels, hold-fasts, gouges, bevelling chisels, centre bits, hatchets, pairs of compasses, pincers, wood-saws. They even possessed a corn-mill made by an Englishman and which Mons. de St Germain had procured for them.

In 1681, Monsieur and Mademoiselle Boisseau, Mons. du Buisson, Monsieur and Mademoiselle de St Denis had given the animals for the agricultural establishment. In the spring of 1690, when the Company of the North took possession again of the farm royal, the Fathers at the Lake farm killed " a cow, a heifer, a large ox, a fat pig four years old, and had also thirteen *minots* (1) of peas, some Indian corn and French wheat, a great quantity of pumpkins, swede and white turnips".

This farm was the Eldorado of the missionaries. They there lodged and fed several old women, widows and children. Charitable souls in Quebec sent them white or Spanish wine, cakes and biscuits, baskets of grapes, of almonds, of Brignolle plums, rice, butter, and cheese which were served to the sick as delicacies.

At the end of the year 1682, the house at Chicoutimi was burnt down and Father Dalmas, who had been residing there took, refuge at the Lake farm.

In 1728, a new church was erected on the picturesque slopes of Chicoutimi and it was there that the scattered remnants of the Métabetchouan neophytes were afterwards collected together. Father Laure's journal tells us how the cross on the new steeple " was saluted with 33 martens by all the Indians and how they

---

(1) An old French measure.

were particularly charmed with the cock ". It has been written somewhere that this church was built on the very spot where Jacques Cartier had encamped, when he made his journey to the Upper Saguenay. This is purely legendary, since neither facts nor any reliable history bear out the assertion.

Mons. Arthur Buies, in his book on the Saguenay, (1) writes :

" At a short distance from the saw-mill at Chicoutimi there was still to be seen, a few years ago, the old mission chapel built by Father Laure in 1728 ; it was bending beneath the weight of years. It was 25 feet long by 15 wide and was built on an eminence overlooking the basin which is at the foot of the falls of the Chicoutimi river. This relic had most touching souvenirs attached to it. Strangers landing at Chicoutimi would hasten to see it, and those who knew something of the old Canadian missions, whatever might be their own form of faith, did not forget to gather up fragments of the stones, &c, belonging to the chapel, that they might carry away a souvenir of it. The tombstone of Father **Coquart**, who died at Chicoutimi, in 1765, was all in pieces, but some parts of the Latin inscription could still be distinguished (1). Some of the sea-captains seemed particularly anxious to collect these remains of a period comparatively recent, but which already seemed distant. The registers, the church-books, the pictures, stones with inscriptions have been lost, for they were left at the mercy of every one in the open chapel.

---

(1) This tomb-stone bore the following inscription: *Tremendum Dei judicium hic in silentio mortis expectat R. P. C. God : Coequart e Socie J. presbyter Montanens : Sylvicol : Mission Obiit Shekuti num IV nona Jul : an 1765.*

(This note was found in a manuscript belonging to Monsieur Faucher, formerly parish-priest of Lotbinière, and we are indebted to the kindness of his nephew, Mons. Faucher de St Maurice, for its reproduction).

In a manuscript of but a few pages, recently discovered by the parish-priest of Chicoutimi in the parish archives and now deposited at the Seminary, it may be seen that, in 1793, the remains of Father Coquart were exhumed. This was done by Monsieur Jean Juste Roy, at that time director of the Quebec Seminary, to whom during the holidays was entrusted the task of visiting the *Postes du Roi* (Royal trading-posts). (For this note, we are indebted to the kindness of Abbé Victor Huart).

Michaux, a celebrated French botanist, at the end of last century, with a view of making a collection of North American plants and flowers, went up the Saguenay as far Lake Mistassini, and he says of this first Chicoutimi chapel: "This building constructed of squared white cedar timber, *thuya occidentalis*, one log resting on another, was still in good preservation, and although these logs had never been covered over, either within or without, I found them so perfectly intact that they had not altered nor shrunk the thickness of half a line during more than sixty years. In the present day we can see the site of this chapel, surrounded by a wooden fence which has been put up by Mr. Price and within which he has had all the sound wood of the chapel buried, so that this last relic of one of the most modest but most interesting of our historical monuments may not be exposed either to the inclemency of the season or the depradations of man. Miss Price has likewise made a sepia sketch of the old chapel and presented it to the bishop's palace at Chicoutimi.

"The old Indian cemetery may be seen beside the fence put up by Mr Price. The cross of the old chapel is in the sacristy of the new Chicoutimi church, and the crucifix is on the altar of the convent there. Lastly, the sacristy door, as also an old cupboard, formerly belonging to the chapel, are preserved at the bishop's palace. This is now all that remain, of the building which heretofore, for nearly a century, had sheltered the Montagnais neophytes who now have nearly entirely disappeared (1).

More fortunate than her prouder rival at Chicoutimi the village of Tadousac has preserved her old chapel.

It stands on the summit of the steep downs that overlook the port. And its pointed steeple, which so long served as a light house to the Saguenay mariner, still bears the cross which the Jesuits planted on it.

---

(1) There still exists in the Paris archives, a memorandum or inventory concerning the Chicoutimi chapel, which inventory was drawn up Oct 8th, 1733.

It is one of the earliest monuments of the Canadian missions.

The primitive Tadousac church was built in 1747, when Monseigneur de Pontbriant was Bishop of Quebec. On March 21st of that year, the carpenter Blanchard set out to go and square the timber of which the church was built, according to the written agreement he had entered into. May 16th, the Jesuit Father Coquart blessed the site where the new church was to be built and hammered in the first peg (1). Hazeur, the farmer of the posts, had paid the expenses of building the church at the Jeremiah Islands. It was to the Intendant Hocquart that Tadousac was indebted for the planks, shingles and all the nails used in the construction of its sanctuary. Wishing to acknowledge this munificence, Father Coquart undertook, for himself and his successors, that Mass should be said on St Anne's day, in Mons. Hocquart's intention, as long as the church existed. The following year, Hocquart

---

(1) Father Coquart's Journal

continued his gifts, and endowed the missionary with 300 livres annually for the use of the church. His successor, Intendant Bigot, did not wish to be outdone in generosity, and, in the autumn of 1749, the Father mentions having received 200 livres with which to finish the roofing.

By June 24th, 1750, the church was completely finished and was valued at 3000 livres by Mons Guillemin, a member of the Council at Quebec and King's Commissioner. The new farmer of the posts, Mons. Hazeur, who had not expended a copper on this edifice, found means of getting himself paid its full value as well as the price of vestments for it. We may be allowed to imagine that Bigot received some gratification on account of this extraordinary reimbursement.

Some years ago, whilst digging beneath the chapel walls, the discovery was made of a plate of lead about six inches square on which the following lines were traced :

L'an 1747, le 16 mai. M. Cugnet, fermier

des postes, F. Doré, commis, Michel Laroye, construisant l'église, le P. Coquart, jésuite. m'a placé.

J. H. S. (1)

(Translation) I was placed here May 16th, 1747, by Father **Coquart**, Jesuit, Mons. Cugnet being farmer of the posts, F. Doré, clerk, Michael Lavoye, builder of the church.

Jesus Saviour of Man.

All that now remains to us as to the origin of the Tadousac chapel is this leaden plate bearing a rough inscription traced by the point of a knife, and some few notes made by Father Coquart.

The old Tadousac chapel has nothing artistic or remarkable in its appearance. The seeker after the architectural beauties or the archeologist will find neither slender towers nor the majestic porticos nor the harmoniously disposed arcades to be found in gothic temples. These simple people, who lived by their hunting and their fishing, attached no glory to raising

---

(1) **Jesu** Homini Salvator.

imposing **edifices.** Capitals and pilasters, festoons or **mouldings,** could they, were they, to be compared with flexible birch bark and fragrant cedar-wood? To the Indian **who** made his dwelling in his **canoe** turned **over** and whose sole pillow was frequently the sand of the seashore, the most simple edifice appeared a marvel, **if only it were** built in the European manner.

The Tadousac church is a very simple structure. It is in the shape of a parallelogram, thirty **feet long** and twenty-five **wide.** Two **narrow windows** open on each **lateral face** at the height of a man from the ground. They light the nave and sanctuary, this **last being finished off in** a semi-circle towards the east. The façade overlooks the bay. From **the** pediment, in which is a large window, **the view is superb.** The roof which is very **high-pitched is** surmounted by a very **humble tower where hangs** the bell which has **seen nearly three centuries of** service, the same bell the sound **of which the** Indians so loved in 1647 and which, after being miraculously saved during the conflagration **of 1661,** has outlived all the vicissitudes of the times. Tradition attributes this to the munificence of the sun-king. The interior of the church is of primitive simplicity and has no architectural ornamentation. The walls, made of solid blocks of cedar, formerly white-washed, are now covered with common papering, in no way recalling the drugget tapestry which was so enthusiastically admired by the Tadousac Indians, two centuries previously.

Having been for a long time abandoned to the care of the poor Tadousac *habitants*, who had no other church, the symmetry of this old chapel has been somewhat destroyed by various additions made to the original structure, which additions might, in their day, have been of some utility, but which the antiquarian will always deplore. Thus the former pointed gable, descending in a straight line to the parapet, has been ornamented with gently curved eaves. This is out of taste. What can be said in favor of the miserable gallery which overshadows the nave or the mean little sacristy which shuts off a part of the apse and spoils its graceful form?

They have made a great mistake in trying to restore this old building and give it a modern aspect. It would have been better not to have attempted repairing the ravages of time.

But let us rejoice that, as **yet,** no vandal has exercised his hammer **in** destroying this venerable old church (1).

Until 1885, **the old** chapel served as a parish-church for the inhabitants of Tadousac. On Christmas-day of that year, Mass was celebrated for **the** first-time in a large church built of stone at a few feet distance from the humble edifice built by the Jesuit Father Coquart. Since that period, it is but once a year, on St Anne's day, that the priest ascends the steps of the old altar before which so many generations have knelt **and where** the praises of God have

---

(1) In 1879 it **was** pitiful to see the state of decay into which the Tadousac chapel had fallen. A Montreal gentleman, Thomas D. King, made an earnest appeal to his fellow-citizens of British **origin.** He published a pamphlet in which **he asked them to make** a subscription in aid of the restoration **of this relic** of the past. This zealous antiquarian's appeal was responded to. He collected sufficient money to enable him to clear the cemetery which was almost entirely neglected. August 7th, 1880, a cross eighteen feet high was erected there.

been sung in the dialects of all the tribes, to the north and south of the Lower St Lawrence. On St Anne's day, the whole parish flocks to the rustic sanctuary to assist at the Mass which is said by the Jesuits' successors, for the intention of Intendant Hocquart, in fulfilment of the promise made two hundred and forty years previously by Father Coquart. The congregation throngs around the edifice, the door of which is left open to enable them to see the priest at the altar. And, on the blue waves of the river, the fishermen who are entering the port respectfully uncover their heads on hearing the silvery sound of the king's bell.

It is thus that the little chapel still raises its head on the Tadousac cliffs, serving as a link to unite one generation with another and thus to hand down to future ages the history of the glorious mission work performed during two centuries.

Be he pious pilgrim or inquiring tourist, whoever lands on the Tadousac shore and visits this venerable ruin, should take care that the preciously guarded relics which are preserved there should be shewn to him. Among these, there are some paintings of the eighteenth century which merit attention. A *Presentation of Mary in the Temple* is signed with the name of Beauvais and bears the date, 1747. This Beauvais was the son of a celebrated engraver and has left some pictures which are much thought of: The *Marriage of Louis XVI and Marie Antoinette* and the *Birth of Louis XVII*. The picture to the left has no name signed, but is very old. The subject is well known. It is a Guardian-Angel conducting a child in the path of virtue and protecting him from a serpent. In the background is seen a chateau lighted up. Probably the painter wished to paraphrase the verse of the Sixteenth Psalm: *Perfect thou my goings in thy paths, that my footsteps be not moved.* Ps: XVI.

Three little pictures representing *Our Lord*, the *Blessed Virgin* and *St Charles Borromeo* were give to the missionary Father Maurice by the Jesuit Father Duplessis. All these paintings date from the first Jesuit missions, and were brought from France, as was also the little Way of the Cross preserved in the chapel. Another of this church's treasures is an *Infant Jesus* in wax, said to have been presented by Louis XIV. This *bambino* is richly dressed and has very red cheeks for his age.

On the altar are two reliquaries bearing the date of 1749, and the relics of St Clement and Saint Prudentia are exposed in them.

In the sacristy may be seen some old wooden candlesticks, roughly carved with a knife, done by the Jesuit Fathers. The massive confessional with its lozenge-shaped gratings was also made by the celebrated Father de la Brosse. We know that the Jesuits often employed their leisure time in doing the humblest sorts of work. Thus Father Maurice, in 1728, gave the first stroke of the axe to the pieces of wood which were to be employed in the construction of the Chicoutimi chapel. It is he who painted the altar-screen, the ceiling, and the beautiful tabernacle; he likewise made some ornaments for the altar, and finished the interior of his house with his own hands for the benefit, he writes, of those who succeed him, asking them to pray for him and wishing them a quieter life. In 1744, we find him again at the Seven Islands, where he was seeing to the squaring of the timber for the chapel. He went into the depths of the forests and wielded the axe in order to encourage his workmen and to have the consolation of having put his hand to the work himself (1).

All these pious souvenirs of the Tadousac chapel are under the charge of the parish-priest. He knows the value of them and watches them as carefully as ever the vigilant dragon watched over the Garden of the Hesperides. There is nothing remarkable in the Tadousac cemetery. It is the God's acre of a country-parish. Some epitaphs are in remembrance of Montagnais Indians. We have sought vainly for the burial place of Mons. de Rochefort, the captain of a French frigate, who died at the entrance of the Gulf, in 1685, on board one of the royal vessels and who was interred in this cemetery.

---

(1) The high-altar in the old Tadousac chapel is of recent origin. It was given by Mrs Connolly, the wife of a Hudson Bay agent,

IX

Father de la Brosse. — History and Legends.

There are some names which need only to be mentioned to evoke the greatest enthusiasm. They seem to vibrate tunefully like the sound of the clarion that calls to battle.

Among the many apostles who have made themselves illustrious in the American missions, there is always some one who has left his mark more particularly on each nation, each tribe. Legends and souvenirs gather thick around these predestined heroes, each one of whom is himself a resumé of a whole period and of the labors performed by twenty or more of his companions. The Micmacs of Acadia have kept the patriarch Maillard in eternal remembrance, the old Abenaquis tribes of Maine still recall the memory of Rasle the martyr, the planters of the Lousiana bayous take off their hats reverently at the name of the missionary Aubry, and the powerful race dwelling on the Lower St Lawrence has not forgotten the Jesuit Father Jean-Baptiste de la Brosse. Of all the missionaries who have exercised their apostleship on the Saguenay shores and in the Gulf regions, it is he who has left behind him the most lively remembrance and who is looked on with the greatest veneration. His name resounds everywhere, in the depths of Lake St John, on the lonely shores of Labrador, in the flourishing villages bordering the river from Cacouna, to the distant confines of Gaspesia and New-Brunswick he is still spoken of. The fisherman taking up his nets, the woodman returning fatigued with his day's toil, the mother beside her child's cradle, the hunter during the long evening halts during his hunting excursions, these all relate wonderful things of the good Father. They all invoke him as a saint in time of misfortune or when the storm is raging on the waters. By the bedside of the sick, the old women often recommend medicaments, the use of which had been taught to their forefathers by the beloved and popular apostle.

The last Jesuit who preached the gospel to the sturdy population of the Gulf, Father de la Brosse forms a sort of keystone to the arch so laboriously erected by the sons of Loyola during the space of two centuries.

We give both the simple history and the gilded legends of this popular hero.

A native of Magnat, a hamlet in the lovely country of Jauldes in Angoumois, the Jesuit Father de la Brosse came to the colony of Canada five years before the English Conquest. At first he filled the office of comptroller in the Quebec college where likewise he was professor of philosophy, but when the enemy came he was already evangelizing the Abenaquis of St Francis of the Lake, a tribe living on the borders of the St John river where he had previously passed a short time in 1755, the year of his arrival. From 1761 to 1766 he resided sometimes at Montreal, sometimes at St Henry of Mascouche where he acted as missionary for nearly five years. By the order of Father Glapion he set out from St Henry de Mascouche to repair to the Tadousac district there to give the finishing touches to the beautiful Montagnais mission. Faith and piety reigned in this favored mission, of which he became the most revered of its many apostles. " May 5th, 1766, at 6 o'c in the afternoon, he " writes on the margin of the Chicoutimi parish-" register I arrived as a missionary at Tadou-" sac, being 42 years and 9 months of age, " having been a priest 13 years, 3 months and " 2 days, having been in Canada 11 years, 10 " months and 5 days, this country having been " subject to the English rule for 5 years, 10 " months and 2 days ".

During an uninterrupted period of sixteen years Father de la Brosse with indefatigable zeal traversed the Montagnais hunting-grounds in every direction, erecting churches, building schools and showing equal zeal in teaching catechism, reading, writing and sacred song. To this very day, Father de la Brosse's teachings are handed down from generation to generation in all the families of the tribe. The old account-books of Quebec's oldest established printer record the wonderful number of books, primers, catechisms, calendars, which he arranged and had published in the Montagnais and Abenaquis idioms, for the use of his neophytes.

He translated the gospel into the Indian dialects. Well versed in the Montagnais language he translated into that idiom all the French writings of his predecessors and collected them all into one volume, together with what he found already written in the native tongue. All these writings he annotated and corrected. In 1770 worn out by four years of incessant labor, he withdrew for a time to the Island of Orleans, where he worked at his Montagnais dictionary which he had commenced on his arrival at Tadousac. For five years more he continued this Benedictine-like undertaking, in the midst of the most perilous journeyings and the most arduous apostolical labors.

The Oblate Fathers, who are now in charge of the northern missions, are said still to possess the Montagnais dictionary at which Father de la Brosse worked for so many years. The greater part of the religious books still in use among the Montagnais were written by him. The bibliographers now vie with each other in securing the primitive editions of the humble missionary's works. The archbishop's library at Quebec contains a copy of de la Brosse's primer, printed in 1767. His catechism and prayer book are extremely rare, only five copies being known to exist.

The good Father de la Brosse, of a gay disposition and possessing ready wit, indulged from time to time in jest and clever repartees. He signed his catechism with his Indian name *Tshitstiisahigan* which means literally *broom* or *brush* (1). In his compilation of his predecessors' writing he has made marginal notes which are sometimes somewhat severe. He excuses himself by saying that he makes these remarks not through ill nature nor to show his wit, but in order to warn the reader against certain errors to be met with. " I only make remarks, he adds, on faults of grammar, leaving aside faults in spelling which the beginners should

---

(1) (*Brosse* is the French for *brush*).

study and which the foolish neglect". *Omissa ortographica cui incipientes student et quam insipientes negligunt.* It is unfortunate that Latin, that language so preeminent for plain-speaking, does not allow us to reproduce this ingenious comparison intact. It was useless for this good Father to deny having any great cleverness, for many anecdotes of his caustic wit are recorded.

On one occasion when he was staying at Chicoutimi, he met with some strangers, tourists whose appearance and ways were anything but admired by the residents at the post. Abusing of the almost boundless liberty which reigned in the establishment and which caused every one's dwelling to be looked on as common property, these gentlemen intruded everywhere and at all hours. They even carried their want of consideration so far as to make endless visits to the missionary, on whom they inflicted a series of the most stupid questions imaginable.

Father de la Brosse, busily engaged with his studies and his labors, had delicately hinted to them that he had but little or no leisure, but these gentlemen paid no heed to what he said. He therefore hit upon a plan for getting rid of his troublesome visitors, thereby showing that he had as much satirical wit in his brain as unbounded goodness in his heart : he wrote the following lines which he fastened to his closed door :

> When a man's busy 'tis really not wise,
> T'inflict on him visits as loafers have done;
> I'd almost as lief that they'd put out my eyes,
> As to spend idle time in paying me one (1).

These verses had the desired effect on the importunate visitors who, finding themselves unwelcome everywhere, relieved Chicoutimi from their disagreeable and pernicious presence.

Wind and rain have carried away the leaf, on which the verse was written, but the verse itself fastened to the door of his little presbytery by Father de la Brosse at the old post of Chicoutimi has been transmitted in more

---

(1) A free translation of Father de la Brosse's lines:
> Pour un homme occupé, rien de plus ennuyeux
> Que de gens désœuvré la visite importune ;
> J'aimerais presqu'autant qu'on me crevât les yeux
> Que de venir ici, pour m'en procurer une !

than one old family. Mons. Joseph-Charles Taché, an ancestor of whom was then a trader at one of the posts, by relating this anecdote in his work *Forestiers et Voyageurs*, has assured its being handed down to posterity.

Father de la Brosse's predecessor in the Tadousac mission, the Jesuit Father Coquart, also made the shores of the Lower St Lawrence resound with the echoes of his muse. In 1757, his brother who was Mayor and Lieutenant General of Police in Paris, presented to the king's ministers some stanzas which the missionary composed in honor of Mons. de Vaudreuil (1).

Father de la Brosse left his mark distinctly on this land of the Saguenay and particularly at Tadousac where he had made his headquarters. His influence spread everywhere that the caprices of commerce and trade had caused posts to be established on the north shore. He moved about incessantly among the rude fishermen and the children of the forest,

---

(1) See *Manuscrits de Québec*, vol. XIII.—March 13th, 1757

confessing and baptizing them and teaching them the doctrine of the one true God. He is to be met with everywhere : at the Bergeronnes, at Escoumains, at the Jeremiah islands, at Seven Islands where he established a school and at his own expense rebuilt the church which Father Coquart had abandoned on account of the crimes of the Indians ; which church had been burnt down by the soldiers during the war. We meet him also at Betsiamits where, during the winter which he passed there, he taught the Indians to read and write, as well as to sing by note. One after the other he visited the distant settlements of Chicoutimi and Lake St John and it was in their mysterious depths that he encountered a group of Naskapis and had the honor of announcing the Word to them the first ; for no missionary had previously been able to penetrate to this tribe.

The Naskapis were very much attached to their superstitions and pagan usages which they did not wish to abandon. It was in vain that Father de la Brosse used every argument in order to convert them. When an Indian is decided on not understanding anything, no one is so deaf as he.

One fine morning a Montagnais, distinguished by his faith and zeal, came to the Father and spoke to him, somewhat as follows.

" Father, the Naskapis have no longer any ears ; but they still have got eyes.

" Well ! replied the Father, what must we show to these poor people ?

I myself do not know ; but, if you could only perform some miracle before them, they would open their eyes and see.

" But I have no power to perform miracles ; that power belongs to God alone.

" What you say is true ; but God sometimes bestows that power : you have often spoken to us of miracles performed by the apostles and other saints.

" It is true I am an apostle ; but, for all that I am only a poor sinner. Besides you know what Our Lord replied to those who asked a miracle of Him : " God does not vouchsafe miracles to those who ask for them ".

The Indian reflected a short time and then replied.

"God does not vouchsafe miracles to those who ask for them, it is true; but he vouchsafes them *sometimes* to those who do not ask for them. The Naskapis have not asked for them, it is I who am asking for them; in that case I must depart: well! I will start at once for Tadousac. God will not vouchsafe a miracle to the one who asks for it; but He will vouchsafe one to those who have not asked for it, but who stand in need of it.... That is right, that is the way of it!"

Whereupon this brave Indian returned at once to his cabin and gave his wife orders to take down the tent, and, carrying his canoe on his shoulders, he hastened the river, and, embarking with all his family, started off for Tadousac.

At that time there was a great drought, and fires raged in the forests; the air was *thick with smoke*; every one felt as if some calamity were impending. Towards noon the flames impelled by the wind and plentifully fed by the dry leaves and branches, commenced to crackle among the tall fir-trees and menaced the cabins with destruction. The Montagnais and Naskapis began removing their belongings out of their huts and were hastening towards a swampy clearing near the Lake, when Father de la Brosse, who was in the midst of them, cried out with a tone of authority which had its effect on them : " Leave your cabins and your goods as they are, touch nothing ; follow me !"

The Naskapis, without considering what they were about, and the Montagnais, inspired with unlimited confidence, accompanied the Father towards the destructive element.

Having arrived at a certain distance from the cabins, the missionary took a stick and traced a line of demarcation, forbidding the fire to pass over it. Then he quietly seated himself on the ground Indian-fashion.

Having reached the place he had indicated the flames seemed to writhe convulsively and then extinguished themselves, as it were, all along the line which the man of God had traced.

The Naskapis, as the Montagnais Indian had said, still had eyes, they opened them and believed in the Word that was preached to them (1).

Father de la Brosse's work was not confined to the missions in the north-east. From the time of the sad drowning of the Recollet Father Ambroise Rouillard, who had charge of the faithful on the right shore of the St Lawrence, all that stretch of country had been without any religious succor, so to speak. In 1771, Father de la Brosse undertook to divide his time between these unfortunate spiritual orphans and his own Montagnais neophytes. From that time forward he might be seen, every year, alternately travelling along the two shores of the river. The French of Cacouna, Ile-Verte, Trois-Pistoles, Rimouski, the Micmacs of Baie des Chaleurs and Ristigouche, the Acadians of

---

(1) We have taken this naive recital from the *Forestiers Voyageurs* of Mons. J. C. Taché.

Bonaventure, Caraquet, Poquemouche, Nipising, Nigasek, Richiboucton, Tracady, in turns profited by his apostolic zeal. At Ristigouche and at Poquemouche, he blessed churches. To all, he taught the elements of grammar and catechism. He confessed, married and baptized them all. When he could not comply with the wishes of these sheep without a pastor, he would write to them and his admirable letters recall the epistles addressed to the early Christian by the apostles. If he met with some child of precocious intelligence, he taught him Latin, directing his studies from afar and interesting himself in the intellectual development of his protégé.

Having terminated his pastoral visit on the right shore, where he had travelled hundreds of leagues, he would embark on some wretched bark and direct his course to the wild shores of Labrador and the Saguenay, where he would stop at each post till he reached Tadousac and where, with all his Indians whom he had appointed to meet him, he would celebrate the feast of St. Anne. It was on this shore on the 26th July, that the Micmacs and Acadians from the Gulf, the Montagnais from the north, the Abenaquis from the south, all might be seen hastening to assist at the annual pilgrimage which had been organized by the indefatigable missionary.

The amount of work performed by this zealous missionary, during his sixteen years' apostolate, is so extraordinary that one might be led to believe it had been exaggerated by romance or legend, did not the registers of the numerous places he visited faithfully record his passage. He has himself left a record of his wanderings written in Latin, wherein he simply and unostentatiously states what he has done. A copy of this itinerary is preciously preserved in the archives of the Quebec archiepiscopal palace, but unfortunately there are but fragments of it remaining and it breaks off suddenly five years before the missionary's death.

Such is the simple history of this apostle who modestly called himself "the 21st pastor of the Montagnais Indians in the posts of the king's domains, of the Society of Jesus".

Father de la Brosse died at Tadousac itself, April 11th, 1782, and the next day the parish-priest of Ile aux Coudres, Mons. Compain, buried him in the mission-chapel where sixteen years previously he had for the first time preached the gospel to the Montagnais.

In the flooring of the sanctuary above his coffin, an opening was made in the shape of a cross, and for a long time after his death, the Indians who went up or down the Saguenay, would never pass the port of Tadousac without landing in order that they might pray in the chapel where the pious missionary's remains were deposited. They would prostrate themselves above the grave and, with their lips pressed to it, would speak to the Father as if he were still living. Then they would place their ear against the opening to listen to the saint's reply. In their artless faith and the simplicity of their hearts they believed that the good Father listened to them from his coffin, that he would reply to their questions and that he would present their petitions to God.

In his life-time, Father de la Brosse had

acquired an extraordinary reputation of sanctity. He even passed for having the gift of prophecy. There is therefore nothing astonishing that the simple-minded populations of those primitive times have surrounded his death with legendary circumstances which are still related around the winter hearth.

When Father de la Brosse died, say the old tales, the bells in all the churches he had served from Bay des Chaleurs up to the head of the Saguenay rang out the death knell, without human intervention. By an inspiration from on High all those who heard the tolling said at once: " Our good Father de la Brosse is dead, he said aright, when on his last visit to us, he told us that we had seen him for the last time, that he would visit our mission no more"!

To make the event still more solemn, it is said that the missionary died precisely at midnight. It is easy to understand how this passing bell sounding during the calm night must have struck the native Indians with astonishment. At least twenty witnesses are cited, bearing testimony to this occurrence. After all

God may have commanded the angel of death to sound the departure of the soul which was ascending to Him after having led so many stray sheep into the right path.

Again, why may not the bells of certain Canadian missions have been endowed, for one day, with the marvellous power of announcing the death of a poor missionary, in the same way as the famous bell at Villela used formerly to ring untouched whenever Spain was threatened by some misfortune and also rang out its mournful knell to announce the death of Ferdinand the Catholic.

The legend goes on to say that Father de la Brosse prophecied the hour of his death. Abbé Casgrain has written a most touching account of what he gathered from the islanders of Ile aux Coudres. We have great pleasure in giving this account to our readers :

"On the evening of April 11th, he says, Mons. Compain, then parish-priest of Ile aux Coudres, was passing the evening alone in his room. After having recited his breviary, said his evening prayers and read his allotted portion, he was quietly studying by the light of his lamp, when suddenly, about midnight, the sound of a bell struck on his ear ringing amid the silence of the night. Filled with astonishment he at first thought himself the victim of an illusion, and approaching the window listened attentively. It was indeed the chapel-bell ringing a passing-bell. Mons. Compain went forth from his presbytery and the bell continued to ring. He entered the chapel and found it empty, but the bell continued still to ring on.

Then a voice sounded in his ear. Did it sound to the ear of the body, or to that of the soul? Who knows! But the voice was distinct and said as follows :

" Father de la Brosse is dead, he has just expired at Tadousac. The passing-bell announces his last sigh. To morrow, go the end of the island. A canoe will come there in search of you and will take you to Tadousac where you will perform the rites of interment for him ".

" The rumor had spread some time previously that, at the moment of Father de la

Brosse's death, the church bells of his missions would announce his decease.

"The next day Mons. Compain was waiting at the lower extremity of the Ile aux Coudres, at the spot where he had been told to wait.

"What had been passing all this time at Tadousac? Father de la Brosse had for some time been on a mission there and was awaiting the arrival of the Indians whom the opening of the navigation would soon see flocking there from the interior. Their canoes laden with furs would descend the Saguenay following the ice as it came down the river.

"During some few weeks the Tadousac rock was the centre of an activity and an amount of trading that contrasted strangely with its solitary and desolate aspect during the rest of the year. The sands of the shore were covered with long files of bark canoes. On the hill-slope the cabins of the Indians were erected one above the other forming an irregular village mostly belonging to the Montagnais tribes. The port of Tadousac was then also filled with mariners from beyond the sea, who touched there.

"Whilst the fur-traders were making their harvesting for the benefit of the great of this world, Father de la Brosse was gathering in his harvest for Heaven from among the little ones of this world.

"Tradition has preserved all the details of his last moments, the circumstances of which were, indeed, of a nature to strike every one.

"On the eve of his death, Father de la Brosse appeared to be in perfect health. He was a large robust, white-haired old man, with an ascetic-looking face and inspired speech.

"During all the day he had been fulfilling the duties of his ministry, confessing, baptizing and praying as usual in the Tadousac chapel.

"At night-fall, he went to take a few hours' recreation at the house of one of the officers of the post. He was as gay and agreeable as ever; he even played a few games of cards with his hosts. Towards nine o'clock he prepared to leave.

"After having said good evening to every

one he was silent for a moment and then, in a solemn tone, said :

"My friends, I bid you farewell, farewell until eternity, for you will not again see me in life. This very evening at midnight *I shall be a corpse*. At that very hour, you will hear my chapel-bell ring : it will announce my death. If you do not believe it you can come and ascertain the fact for yourselves. But I ask of you not to touch my body. To morrow, you will go to Ile aux Coudres to fetch Mons. Compain to enshroud me and perform the rites of sepulture. You will find him waiting at the end of that island. Do not fear to embark, whatever may be the weather. I answer for the safety of those who set out on this journey".

"At first they thought that the Father was jesting, but he insisted on what he had said with such an air of conviction and of authority that there was no room left for doubt.

"One of the men employed at the post remonstrated with him, saying : " Father, you appear to be in perfect health and your face shows no sign of suffering. How then can you believe your end to be so nigh?

"My child, he replied, by the end of the day you will know that my words are true. And he left the house.

"After his departure the company he had left remained quite stupefied, not being able to believe in the reality of his prophecy.

"Those who had watches placed them on the table and awaited the result in great anxiety. Ten o'clock struck, then eleven, then midnight, and then the chapel-bell began to sound.

"With one accord, they all rose and, impelled by sudden fear, hastened to the chapel. They entered.

"By the faint light of the sanctuary lamp they perceived Father de la Brosse's black robe in the choir. He was stretched motionless on the ground, his face bowed down on his clasped hands which rested on the lowest altar step.

"He was dead.

"This strange news spread like wild-fire through the mission. At daybreak the whole population of Indians and whites rushed to the chapel. Each one wished to gaze once more on the saint who was stretched before them lifeless. No one dared touch him. With mingled feelings of grief and admiration they gazed on him, prayed and invoked him. Tears flowed from every eye.

"During the whole day, the crowd silently came and went in the chapel, they not being able to tear themselves from the sight of the holy missionary who had so often made that very sanctuary resound with his brilliant and touching exhortations. The Indians remained there motionless for hours, one finger pressed to their lips, expressing by this gesture that no words could do justice to their heartfelt grief.

"In the meanwhile, on that very morning, a south-east wind had sprung up and raged with such violence that the river was covered with snowy-crested waves. Nobody dared to launch a boat on such a sea. On seeing this the head-officer of the post said to those near him:

"Are there some three men among you

brave enough to accompany me in accomplishing the last desire of our good Father? Remember what he said : "I answer for the safety of those who set out on this journey".

"A canoe is launched; the four men who embark in it put out to sea. Hardly have they left Tadousac when, to their extreme surprise, the water becomes smooth before them.

"Whilst all around the tempest raged with fury, the sea being white with foam, an invisible hand urged them rapidly along, so that by eleven o'clock in the morning they rounded Goose Cape (Cap aux Oies) and came in sight of Ile aux Coudres.

"Mons. Compain was awaiting them at the lower end, walking about the rocks with a book in his hand. As soon as they were within sound of his voice, he cried out to them :

"Father de la Brosse is dead, you have come to fetch me for his interment. The canoe approached the shore, Mons. de Compain embarked in it and, on the evening of that same day, he landed at Tadousac".

Such is the marvellous legend which is

related by the Ile aux Coudres people and which is repeated constantly by the colonists on the Lower St Lawrence.

It is said that old soldiers, who have a thousand times braved death on the battlefield, weep when they think they may be obliged to die quietly in their beds like ordinary people suffering from gout or helplessly paralyzed. Even those who read the life of some illustrious warrior love to picture to themselves that he will fall like a hero at the head of his troops. The missionary and the soldier resemble one another, they are of one family. Their life has been similarly of devotedness and sacrifice and legends love to surround them with a halo of glory. We love this sweet popular legend which makes Father de la Brosse die so valiant, so lovely, a death on the altar steps amidst the solemn stillness of the night. It is just such a death as we would dream of for this apostle. Alas! why is it that stern reality must need destroy the web woven by poetical legendaries and which our ancestors have so firmly believed in from their very childhood?

Father de la Brosse did not die at midnight in the solitude of the sanctuary, nor did he tell the canoe-men to go on their way fearlessly and brave the tempest in order to seek the Ile aux Coudres parish-priest to enshroud him. Here is how the authentic act of sepulture runs, telling us with prosaic conciseness what was the end of the missionary :

" April 12th, one thousand seven hundred and eighty-two, was buried in the church of this mission the body of Jean Baptiste de la Brosse, missionary priest of the Company of Jesus, who died the previous day at $\frac{1}{2}$ p. five in the evening, fortified with the sacraments of Penance and Extreme Unction, aged fifty-eight years. Were present Charles Brassard and others, all of whom declared themselves unable to sign this paper according to what is required by the regulations.

(Signed) P. J. Compain, Priest (1).

---

(1) Extract from the register of baptisms, marriages and deaths of the Indians and others residing in the mission of the king's domain.

No matter, in spite of this yellow leaf taken from a dusty register, the missionary work of Father de la Brosse remains in all its entireness. The dreamy legend, so long accredited, is proved untrue, but time can never destroy the memory of his works nor of his ardent apostolical zeal.

The following lines have embodied the legend we have given above and we think our readers will thank us for introducing them to their notice.

They are from the elegant pen of Professor Caven, of the Prince of Wales' College, Charlottetown, Prince Edward Island:

THE BELL OF DEATH

A Legend of Tadousac and Ile aux Coudres.

1 Fierce blew the strong south-eastern gale,
   The sea in mountains rolled,
   A starless sky-hung wildly tossed,
   The midnight hour had tolled.

2 Is that a sea — is this an hour,
   With sky so wildly black,
   To launch a bark so frail as that,
   Ye men of Tadousac?

3 **Strong** though your arms, brave though your hearts,
　As arms and hearts can be,
　That tiny skiff can never **live**
　In such a storm-swept **sea.**

4 Where Saguenay's dark waters roll
　To swell St Lawrence **tide,**
　Down to the beach that stormy night
　Four stalwart fishers stride.

5 On through **the surf** the frail boat speeds,
　And see, before her prow,
　The giant waves sink down and crouch
　As if in homage low.

6 Calm as the surface of a lake
　Sunk deep mid wooded hills
　The track spreads out before the boat,
　The sail a fair breez fills.

7 While all around the angry waves
　Bear high their foamy scalps,
　And frowning hang like toppling crags,
　O'er passes through the Alps.

8 Who stilled the waves on Gallilee
　Makes smooth that narrow track,
　'T is faith that makes your hearts so bold,
　Ye men of Tadousac?

・・・・・・　・・

9 Fierce blows the strong south-eastern-gale
　Around the lowly pile
　Where dwells the lonely missioner
　Of Coudres' grassy isle.

10 His psalms are read—his beads are said ;
    And by the lamp's pale beam,
    He studious culls from sainted page
    Sweet flowers on which to dream.

11 But see he starts ! strange accents come
    Forth from the flying rack:
    "Funeral rites await your care,
    Haste on to Tadousac ?

12 And from the church's lowly spire
    Tolled forth the passing-bell,
    And far upon the tempest wing
    Was borne the funeral knell.

13 That night along St Lawrence tide
    From every church's tower
    The bells rang forth a requiem
    Swung by some unseen power.

. . . .

14 The storm has lulled and morning's light
    Pierces the shifting mists,
    That hang like shattered regiments
    Around the mountain crests.

15 From brief repose, the anxious priest
    Forth on his mission speeds
    O'er pathless plains, by hazel brake,
    Where the lone bittern breeds.

16 At length upon the eastern shore
    Ended his weary track,
    Where wait the hardy fishermen,
    The men from Tadousac.

17 " Heaven bless you" cried the holy man,
 "I know your high behest,
 God's friend, and your's and mine has gone
 To claim his well-earned rest ".

18 Unmoor the boat; spread out the sail,
 And, o'er a peaceful track,
 Again, in eager flight, the boat
 Shoots home to Tadousac.

19 Before the altar, where so oft
 He broke the Holy Bread,
 Clasping the well-worn crucifix
 The priest of God lay dead.

20 It was a solemn sight, they say,
 To see the cold calm face
 Upturned beneath the sanctuary light
 Within that holy place.

21 Happy La Brosse ! to find for judge
 Him, whom from realms above
 Thy voice had called to dwell with men
 A prisoner of love !

In the peaceful hamlets bordering the right bank of the river St Lawrence, for many a day will be recounted the simple legend of the silver goblet which Sieur Rioux had lent to the good Father and which the latter had promised, living or dead, to return to him. This goblet was found one day on the floor of the large hall in the manor-house, without anybody being able to say how it had come there. For many a day will the peasants of Trois-Pistoles show a rock on the edge of the sea bearing the impress of the knees and the snow-shoes of the popular missionary. For many a day, too, will the Ile Verte folks speak of the miracles which he accomplished in their midst. For many a long day will the Gulf sailors, mingling his memory with that of a brave parish-priest, relate how he confounded the *Braillard de la Madeleine*, * whose frightful lamentations might be heard far out at sea.

Happy are the people who still believe in these lovely and holy legends!

We do not know why it was long believed that the remains of **Father** de la Brosse had been removed from the Tadousac chapel and placed in the Chicoutimi church. The oldest inhabitants of Tadousac, when questioned on

---

(1) See note at end of chapter.

the subject, always confidently affirmed that they had never heard of this translation, and they could remember as far back as fifty years or more. If such an event had taken place, it could not have escaped their attention. In the year (1888), researches were made which resulted in the discovery of a coffin placed in the exact place where the priest stands at the commencement of Mass. Since tradition informs us that the missionary's body was buried under the altar-steps, opposite to the tabernacle, we were evidently standing in the presence of the venerable remains of Father de la Brosse. In this cedar coffin, which was in tolerable preservation, there remained only a few bones which immediately crumbled into dust. For more than a century the mortal remains of the last Jesuit Saguenay missionary had been reposing in the Tadousac chapel. It was on the occasion of the discovery of this tomb that some members of the clergy caused the following inscription to be placed in the choir of the old sanctuary where it is still to be seen :

D. O. M. (1)

A LA MÉMOIRE

DU

R. P. J. B. de la BROSSE,

dernier missionnaire jésuite de Tadousac,

MORT EN ODEUR DE SAINTETÉ

A L'AGE DE 58 ANS

Inhumé dans la chapelle de Tadousac,

LE 12 AVRIL 1872.

Quem speciosi pedes evangelizantium pacem.

Rom. i. 15

(1) Translation : **To the memory of the Rev. Father Jean Baptiste de la Brosse, last Jesuit missionary of Tadousac, who died in the odour of sanctity, at the age of 58 years and was buried in the chapel of Tadousac, April 12th, 1872.**

---

* We think our English and American readers will like to hear something about this *Braillard de la Madeleine or Magdeleine*; we therefore take the following account of it from the Chronicles of the St Lawrence by the celebrated Canadian littérateur and naturalist, J. M. LeMoine Esq. of Spencer Grange, near Québec, the author of many most interesting works both in French and

English. "A local *cicerone's* account of the phenomenon is as follows: An awful shipwreck once occurred at this place. A father and mother, amongst crowds of others, here found a watery grave. Their infant son, by some miraculous interposition of his guardian angel, was safely washed ashore. The darling boy was safely landed on the pebbly beach, and soon made it vocal with his grief and moans for the loss of his best friends. His infant wailings, blended with the swelling storm, struck the ears of some belated fisherman whose boat was passing the entrance of the River Magdeleine. Hence the name *Le Braillard de la Magdeleine*. The noise is still heard in stormy weather and may be explained either by the action of the surf rolling into one of the many hollow caverns along the Gaspé coast, and which has astonished all observers, or by shelving rocks over which it moans like an unquiet spirit.... The moanings of the *Braillard* might be caused by the action of high winds on two large pines which overhang a neighboring cape, and whose trunks grate ominously on one another. Abbé Ferland, the Canadian historian, writes thus of the Braillard :" Where is the Canadian sailor, familiar with this coast, who has not heard of the plaintive sounds and doleful cries uttered by the *Braillard de la Magdeleine*?.... Is it the soul of a shipwrecked mariner asking for Christian burial?.... Is it the voice of the murderer condemned to expiate his crime on the very spot which witnessed its commission? For it is well known that Gaspé wreckers have not always contented themselves with robbery and pillage......or is this the celebrated Devil's Land mentioned by the cosmographer Thevet where, according to him, Roberval (in 1562) abandoned his niece la Demoyselle Marguerite with her lover and with her old Norman duenna?" ...Abbé Casgrain tells a tale about the *Braillard* in which a bad priest became, through grief, reduced to a skeleton, for having refused to christen a child, who subsequently died unbaptized and was heard to moan constantly afterwards. The reader can make choice of one of these explanations.

THE TRANSLATOR.

X

What has become of the aborigenes. — The doom of the Mamelons — What modern Tadousac is like. — The ambition of the Tadousacians. — Seaport and winter navigation. — Sea-bathing and tourists. — A walk round the neighborhood of Tadousac. — The encroaching sands. — Fatalism. — The Baude mill and its marbles.

There have been three Romes, and there have been three Tadousacs : that of the Indians, that of the traders and that of the settled colonists. By a strange destiny this capital of an immense kingdom where twenty nations established their temporary dwelling, this renowned trading-depot which attracted all the European fleets sent out to North America by the old country, was never more than a simple village in the past and is but a little hamlet at present.

A " Relation " of 1646 tells us that formerly there dwelt on the shores of this port 300 hunters and warriors who, with their families, made a total of about fifteen hundred souls. During the trading season some 1000 or 1200

Indians would land on that shore (1). **God's praises were sung there in twenty different languages** (2).

Race succeeded race as one wave follows another. To make room for new comers destiny decreed that **whole tribes should be carried off by implacable epidemics.** In 1670, for example, the small-pox **decimated** Tadousac **so that the village was nearly entirely** abandoned.

War did the rest. When Champlain **arrived in this port,** he found the Indian natives celebrating a great victory they had just gained over the Iroquois. The Tadousacians by persuading the French to take part in their long-standing quarrels nearly caused the loss of the colony and they themselves finished by paying dear for the vain glory of having gained some passing **victories.** The Iroquois tracked them mercilessly. **In** vain did they take refuge in the deepest recesses **of** their forests and, even at the North sea, they were **pursued** and mas-

---

(1) Garneau, v. I. p. 220.

(2) Relation 1652.

sacred. Traces of the savage Iroquois may be found everywhere in those parts. The shores of Lake St John have them in eternal remembrance. Two miles before coming to St Félicien, one of the most distant parishes of that far-off region, the traveller will be surprised to learn that a peaceful little river which he is crossing bears the name of the Iroquois. Quite recently a great number of arrows and tomahawks were found on its fertile banks.

After having ascended the river Assamachouanne to its source, Father Druillettes had to turn back. A band of Iroquois had gone on ahead and were awaiting him. Father Albanel, during his great journey to the North sea in 1672, also found vestiges of a fort and entrenchments made by the Iroquois the year that they had massacred twenty tribes who had been living peacefully and unsuspectingly in those regions.

The Montagnais Indians had also other bitter enemies in the tribes from Gaspesia and also in the Acadians, to both of whom they bore mortal hatred (1). The Esquimaux, in their turn, swarmed down from their lonely lands in north Labrador and overwhelmed the Montagnais, causing their nearly complete ruin.

An ancient legend says that the homeric combat, in which the Montagnais were overpowered by the Esquimaux and fell never to rise again, was fought on the Tadousac doons, to the solemn accompaniment of a tremendous earthquake which shook these shores to their very foundations, precipitating high mountains into the sea and completely changing the face of the country.

An American writer (2) has composed a book on this tragic circumstance, entitled *The Doom of Mamelons*. It is an obscure sort of fiction, badly put together, most improbable and not particularly well written. It is sold on board the steamboats and at the railway stations.

There are now but a few scattered rem-

---

(1) Relation of 1635.
(2) Mr. W. H. Murray

nants of the great Christian Montagnais tribe remaining. Some of them live at Betsiamites under the charge of the Oblate Fathers : this is their principal centre. Others have pitched their tents on the banks of Lake St John. One by one they are falling victims to that terrible disease, *phthisis*; and they are slowly and stoïcally dying out.

For the last thirty years Tadousac has had **no other history** than that of the patient, hardworking settlers who have been trying to cultivate successfully the sand and ungrateful soil. **There are some** twenty-five farmers who are working there, enduring great hardship and straining every nerve to succeed. Wheat, rye, barley, oats, peas, are **sown** there. Some of the land **is** favorable to **the** cultivation of hay and good **crops** of potatoes are grown, the soil being adapted to them. It is during the first fortnight **in May that the crops are** put in and they are **housed in the** beginning **of September.** It is said that the crops are satisfactory when the season is favorable.

The mission of Tadousac comprises an area

of 8,624 acres, divided into 107 lots, of which about a third are unfit for cultivation. An agent of the Crown Lands is resident there to grant farms along the sea-line of the North coast, to those who are courageous enough to undertake them. In 1888, four concessions were made.

The fixed population of Tadousac consists of 590 souls belonging to 106 families (1).

The smaller number farm ; the rest mostly labor either as day-laborers or as shanty-men. About fifteen are occupied in the coasting-trade. Lastly, as in all well organized parishes, each trade has its representative. A small group forms what may be called the official personages : the district-magistrate, the Crown Lands agent, the director of the fish-breeding establishment, and the doctor. Formerly there was a resident Custom House officer, but on the

---

(1) In all there are 91 households. An exact census divides the population as follows: 25 farmers, 15 navigators, 23 hunters, 3 merchants, 6 carpenters, 2 blacksmiths, 1 shoemaker, 2 masons, 4 carters, 1 baker, 1 miller, 1 pilot, 1 doctor, 1 district-magistrate, 1 post-master and telegraph operator, 1 Crown Lands agent.

death of that gentleman he was not replaced. The hunters form a most interesting caste : we will speak of them further on.

Apart from the artificial salmon-breeding, Tadousac has no special industry. Formerly there was a saw-mill, which, it is said, was the first of the kind ever established on the shores of the Saguenay, but it exists no longer. Larousse, the encyclopedist, states that at Tadousac there is a considerable trade in woolen materials. We must humbly confess that we ourselves have never seen a single sheep there.

Nowhere can there be found a more hospitable, affable or courteous people than those of Tadousac. The live uprightly and honorably, being content with little.

In summer it is pleasant enough living there, but in winter there is a terrible feeling of isolation. The mail arrives regularly four times a week, and may be looked on as the only amusement or distraction that is to be had.

When the North wind blows each one

retires into his well warmed house and there waits patiently.

The climate is not more rigorous at Tadousac than elsewhere. We have before us the table of meteorological observations for the first three months of 1889 and we there see that its average temperature can bear favorable comparison with that of many more inland localities.

In winter, the entrance to the River Saguenay and the Bay of Tadousac are as free from ice as in the summer (1). When there is an east wind for several consecutive day, shoals of ice come down which disappear when the north-west wind commences to blow. This ice is not solid and hard like fresh-water ice, but crumbles away easily in the rays of the sun.

Twice only, in the memory of man, has the Saguenay opposite Tadousac been covered with a compact sheet of ice. The first time, about twenty-four years ago, an ice-bridge formed and lasted for a month and a half On a second

---

(1) In the winter the Saguenay is covered with ice as far as the St Louis Islands, nineteen miles above Tadousac.

occasion, about fifteen years ago, the cold suddenly formed a path from one shore to the other, which path lasted about three weeks. Since that time the phenomenon has not recurred.

It has often occurred that vessels setting out from Quebec late in the autumn have been caught in the river-ice and forced to take refuge in Tadousac harbor, where they have passed the winter in safety (1).

It is one of the glories of Tadousac that in winter its superb bay is not covered with an icy winding-sheet, as is often the case with many highly valuable ports.

Those who have tried to solve the problem of winter-navigation on the river St Lawrence have always looked on Tadousac Bay as the great port of safety for northern navigators. The last report of the Quebec Geographical Society contains a letter from the agent of the

---

(1) Amongst others we may cite the *Pride of England* which Captain Lecours ran into Tadousac in the middle of the month of February, 1871. The same navigator, in the middle of December, 1874, ran the bark *Resene* into the port of Tadousac.

Minister of Marine in that city, in which it is said that the greatest obstacle to winter navigation on the river St Lawrence is the absence of harbors of refuge, in the case of vessels being overtaken by dark nights or snow-storms, but that Tadousac would be an excellent port for vessels in distress, as they could anchor there during any kind of weather.

Father Lacasse, the Oblate missionary, who has long dwelt on the coast of Labrador, when questioned by the Canadian Government who were desirous of ascertaining whether any winter port was to be met with on the North shore, unhesitatingly replied that Providence had formed Tadousac Bay for that express purpose. In his opinion, winter navigation will sooner or later be established, and it is only a question of time. Often, he writes, (1) when travelling on my snow-shoes from one place to another along those shores, I have contemplated the sea which in January and February is free from ice and I say to myself, if those who hold the destinies of

---

(1) *A mine producing gold and silver* (1880) p. 162 and following.

the country in their hands only saw what I see now, behold what efforts would they not make to utilize these advantages for establishing winter-navigation?

When Father Lacasse wrote these lines, the press and the politicians were discussing what line it would be most advantageous to adopt for the projected railroad between Quebec and Lake St John. He took an animated part in the debate, asking that Tadousac might be chosen as the terminus. According to him nothing could be easier than, when once the road was opened to Lake St John, to continue it to Chicoutimi and thence to Tadousac, along the sides of the mountains and through the valleys of the St Margaret river and the Baude mill. By adopting this line, he added the interests of all will be protected and we can enjoy a winter-port, an object of prime importance for the prosperity of the country.

After having discussed distances, the winds and currents, this intelligent and devoted missionary, carried away by his enthusiasm, predicted that one day Tadousac would become the New-York of Canada. "Tadousac, he writes, is the terminus of the Atlantic by sea, and will be the terminus of the Pacific by land.

"The first vessels that bore our forefathers hither halted at Tadousac, *the end of the sea* before going up the rivers. Tadousac was then the first landing-place from the old world. It was there that for two centuries the old and new worlds met ; it was there that the first Mass was celebrated in Canada and that the Creator of the world came in person to take possession of his domain. How admirable are the ways of Providence ! It is there that, two centuries and a half later, the new world will hasten to meet the old. The question is asked, where will be the capital city of the *Dominion*, i. e. the town which will be the commercial centre of a country larger than Europe, of a country counting more than five million souls ? Will it be Toronto ? Ottawa ? Montreal ? Quebec ? Halifax ? Those who will come after us, urged thereto by what politicians call the force of circumstances, which we call God's providence, will reply with one accord : Tadousac is the capital city of the *Dominion*.

"This is no mere dream. What was Chicago when our fathers were born ? What was Winnipeg, only a few years ago ?" (1)

Mr. Arthur Buies, who has just written a book on the *Upper Ottawa*, also predicts that one day the valleys of the Saguenay and of the St Maurice will be united by a railway, with three branch-lines leading respectively to the Pacific on the west, to James' Bay on the north, and to the port of Tadousac on the east (2).

As we see, the peaceful hamlet of Tadousac has zealous advocates, and many who are worthy of credence predict for it a glorious future. How know we that these dreams will not be realized ? Two centuries ago, was it not at Tadousac that all the fur-trade of half North America was carried on ?

Were not canoes arriving on its shores from Nipissing, Temiscamingue, Abitibbi and

---

(1) ibid p. 175.
(2) p. 305.

the celebrated North sea? When engineers shall be digging the foundations for their steel rails, they will find traces of the old hunting paths of extinct races.

Whilst waiting for the rising sun of these days, Tadousac contents itself with being one of the most charming watering-places to be found in Canada.

It would indeed be a pity to see its fine sands defiled by the heavy engines of modern civilization. Can one possibly imagine that one day all these villas, now so coquettishly hidden away in the cliffs' windings, will be replaced by dirty, foul-smelling workshops, whose tall chimneys will raise their heads prosaïcally towards the pure and limpid firmament?

Before the fulfilment of these predictions made by the party of progress, before this enchanting hamlet of Tadousac disappears forever from our sight. let us examine it as it now stands, as the tourists and the summer visitors have fashioned it.

About twenty years ago some English

shipowners of Quebec and Montreal, in search of watering-places, discovered Tadousac. A joint stock company with a capital of $40,000 was formed to turn this lovely country to account (1).

A large hotel was built, and, thanks to judicious advertising, tourists flocked there from all parts. Since then Tadousac has always retained its good name, and no distinguished traveller, visiting the St Lawrence bathing-places, fails to pass at least some few days on these enchanting shores.

In the time of Lord Dufferin, who here built himself a costly and handsome residence opposite to the Bay, Tadousac ranked very high among fashionable resorts. At the present time Tadousac is held in special esteem by artists during their country repose, when they flee from the noisy crowd that frequents ordinary bathing-places.

The hamlet of Tadousac has only one hilly,

---

(1) Tadousac Hotel and Sea-bathing Company (1865-29 Vict. ch. 93).

sandy street, which is frequented by the visitors on the arrival or departure of the boats. During the bathing-season, **every** one is to be seen on the Bay, whence there **is** a splendid view. When the tide goes down, no boulevard can be compared with this picturesque shore, carpeted by fine soft sand. At high water, the port is filled with little **boats and** the rhythmical splashing of the **oars** blends with the most charming boating-songs. In this lovely and sheltered bay, a child **can** row **a canoe**, the sea is always so calm. Children of twelve may be seen sturdily rowing like old sailors.

The tourists' spacious hotel surrounded by roomy verandahs **is** situated on the top of the cliff. Smiling villas, half-hidden **in** green thickets, surround it. **In the** midst of all these sumptuous dwellings may be seen Father Coquart's **chapel**, a century old. How many tourists **who have** set out on the round **Saguenay** trip have stopped several days on **the Tadousac** shores in order **to** examine more minute**ly this** relic of the **past**! How many, who only come to throw a passing glance, have lingered here for long, attracted by the beauty of the landscape!

The environs of Tadousac are barren enough, but the little corner where the hamlet itself is situated is so lovely and the views from it so beautiful that the tourist is perfectly satisfied.

Those, however, who are somewhat acquainted with the history of the country, do not fail to push on to Baude mill to see the marbles mentioned by the old writers.

A distance of three miles separates Baude mill from Tadousac, and the road leading to the former place is a regular desert of sand. On turning Cow Point, which shelters the port from the sea-winds, one is surprised to find that the green, round-headed mountains (mamelons) one has left behind are succeeded by a desolate and barren plain, destitute of all vegetation. Formerly there were good farms here where wheat grew plentifully. To the east of Cow Point is shewn the place where formerly the Jesuit missionaries had their agricultural establishment. Only about fifty years ago flower-plants, rose-trees, and fruit-trees were found in abundance at the spot known by the name of *The Jesuits' Garden*. Now there is nothing left there, and the shore has been half-washed by the sea. Everything has disappeared.

The wind, a most tempetuous one, is incessantly sweeping over this shore, carrying everything before it. Grass will not grow where Attila's horse has trod. Here, gaps have been made, trees have been violently twisted and uprooted, houses have been swallowed up. Then there remained nothing but sand, arid sand, covering the whole plain. The sand has invaded the whole shore, swallowing it up; Victor Hugo would say : a sepulchre has risen like a tide from the depths of the earth and crept onwards towards the living. It is said that the wind has already hollowed out about twenty feet of the shore and every year makes an average inroad of another foot.

From the top of the rocks surrounding Tadousac, these ravages of the wind and sea are to be seen plainly. An inhabitant of the village points out the spot where the old house of his ancestors used to stand. Only a few stones remain to show where it once stood. They had had to flee, as others had done before them, they had had to abandon the fields where their life had passed so sweetly and happily : *campos ubi Troja fuit.*

And the good man in order to explain this phenomenon of the sea invading the land, which had been imprudently stripped of its wood, told us that this misfortune *had to happen* since it had been foretold.

We were far from expecting to meet with a Musulman fatalist in the peaceful hamlet of Tadousac, but *it was written,* no doubt. *Kismet, it is fate.*

The road leading to Baude mill crosses the desolate country we have been describing. The spectacle, beheld by the tourist on arriving at his destination, is not of a nature to efface the impression produced by the previous portion of his pilgrimage.

Charlevoix relates that, on arriving at Baude mill in 1720, he asked to see it, and that they showed him some rocks from which issued a stream of clear water. "At last there is wherewithal, said he, to construct a water-mill, but it does not look much as if one would ever be built". Father Charlevoix' prediction was not fulfilled. On these barren rocks a mill has been built, but its owner does not appear to have made his fortune, if one may judge by the ruined dikes and the miserable look of the whole establishment. The mill-stones are turned by the thread-like stream of water supplied by the brook of Baude mill, which brook is often dry. Yet such as at is, this mill suffices to grind the small amount of wheat grown on this barren, ungrateful soil.

Whence comes the name of Baude's mill which has been given to this barren spot, since the first foundations of New France were laid? Champlain and the writers who succeeded to him speak of the Baude mill, without troubling themselves to tell us its history. This place was formerly the roadstead of Tadousac." For the anchorage to be good, Baude mill must be in sight, writes the founder of the colony. It is a spring of water coming from the mountains; you should anchor near it".

According to the tradition of the country people, the left shore of the stream which runs to Baude's mill was formerly terminated by a long point of land stretching into the water and forming a natural bay. Two isolated rocks were at the end of this little peninsula and were called by the sailors *bonhomme* and *bonne femme Baude*. We give the legend for what it is worth.

Have the sea and wind eaten away this tongue of land? Did it disappear in some cataclysm of nature? This is a mystery. In the opinion of several geologists (1), the physiognomy of all this coast has been changed by the violent shocks of the celebrated earthquake of 1663.—The historian Parkman relates (2) that

---

(1) Among others Mr Sterry Hunt.

(2) *Old Regime in Canada* p. 127.

some fishermen, who were descending the river in a skiff, found their progress suddenly impeded, near Tadousac, by a high mountain covered with trees being precipitated into the water at a few yards from them.

However this may be, the Baude mill which was formerly so renowned as a place of anchorage no longer offers any shelter to the mariner.

That which has most contributed to making the Baude mill known is that all the old writers have stated that the rocks surrounding it are of marble. Nothing further was necessary to stimulate the greed of speculators. Unfortunately, it has been found, on closer examination, that the few white veins which may be seen running through the sides of the rocks are not of a nature to repay the cost of working. This marble easily crumbles on being exposed to the air and at most could only be applied to a few ornamental purposes.

This is about all that can be seen during an hour's excursion by the tourist who is anxious to become acquainted with the neighborhood of Tadousac. If he does not care to traverse anew the lonely plain leading to Baude mill, he has only to follow the rugged road which winds along the stream turning the mill-wheel. Its meanderings will lead him, sometimes through wood, sometimes by mountain and valley, up to the summit of the mountain which overlooks the back part of Tadousac, whence there is a splendid view of the whole region. This is called *going round the Concession*. Making this tour is like visiting the Park or the Bois. It is the fashionable excursion of the place.

XI

Hunting and fishing. — Ichthyological establishment. — Artificial salmon-breeding. — Sea-trout. — Fishing in the lakes. — Seal fishing.

We cannot take leave of Tadousac, which for nearly three centuries was the great hunting and fishing centre of North America, without speaking a little of the hunting and fishing still to be found there. Alas! they are but a shadow of what formerly were to be met with; yet such sportsmen as are attracted by the rugged and wild aspect of our northern countries will not fail to visit this place formerly so celebrated. Whilst their families can remain at the large Tadousac hotel, they can go and pass two or three weeks salmon-fishing on the rivers which discharge into the Saguenay.

Since 1875, there has been an ichthyological establishment at Tadousac for the reproduction of that royal denizen of our waters, the salmon. It is installed at *Anse à l'Eau*, precisely where our great exporter of Saguenay timber, Mr Price, had built the first saw-mill of this region.

There is no more interesting way of passing the time than that of visiting this piscicultural establishment.

The salmon for breeding purposes are taken in nets at the fishing-places, two miles from the establishment. One of these fisheries is on the shore, opposite to the old farm of the first Tadousac missionaries and is still called the Jesuits' fishery.

The fish for breeding are set free in a pond where the tide is let in by means of a grating made of stakes high enough to prevent the fish escaping. The spawning-season generally lasts from Oct. 20th to November 10th. When it is approaching, the colours of the salmon become brighter, the edges of their fins become empurpled and red spots are perceived on the back of the fish. The males and females are then separated from each other and placed in special reservoirs and the work of manipulation commences.

Nothing is more simple to those who, through practice, have acquired great skill in performing the manipulation. The operator carefully takes hold of the female, taking care if the fish be very big to wrap her up in a cloth. He lightly passes the inside of his thumb or of two fingers over the belly without pressing too hard. If the eggs are mature they will thus be expelled, but, if they are not quite mature, a certain resistance is felt which must not be overcome; the female should then be put back into the reservoir to await a more propitious time.

Naturalists calculate that each female produces about as many thousands of eggs as the parent herself weighs pounds. The official head of the establishment at Tadousac (1) says that a female generally gives from 600 to 700 eggs per pound of her own weight. A female of 20 lbs would therefore yield 12,000 or more eggs.

---

(1) M. L. Catellier.

The fecundation is performed immediately after the eggs are laid. For this purpose a male is taken and the milt is made to flow on the eggs in the same manner and with the same precautions as have been taken with the female.

When the manipulation is finished, the salmon are thrown back into the pond where they continue to do perfectly well. Towards the middle of November the gates of their prison are opened and they return to the sea.

They say that some of the fish appear to regret leaving the temporary abode constructed for them and supported through the paternal solicitude of the Government. For long they return and with their pointed snouts seem to be smelling at the gently sloping embankment which separates them from the moist cradle where the paste was so tender and so regularly distributed.

When once the eggs are fertilized, they are carefully placed in the hatching apparatus on hurdles covered with a thin layer of gravel (1). These hurdles are inserted in wooden troughs through which incessantly flows a large thread of clear, limpid water coming from that lake which Champlain found so charming and which can be perceived in the hollow of the mountain, two or three arpents from the piscicultural establishment.

This water is maintained at the temperature of 34 degrees during the whole period of incubation. It is during this period that the most constant and minute precautions have to be taken, in order to remove the bad eggs, to regulate the stream of water and to let nothing impair its purity. Neither is it a small task preserving the eggs from the diseases to which they are liable and to protect them against the parasites which try to prey on them.

The space of from a month and a half to two months must elapse before the eggs are hatched and the young fry commence eating six weeks afterwards. The spring-time is the

---

1) In the autumn of 1888, 1,685,000 eggs were thus deposited at Tadousac.

period chosen for distributing these young fry among the great tributaries of the Saguenay and certain lakes which flow into the river by gently descending streams, so as to facilitate the descent of the young salmon to the sea.

From 1875 to 1888, 10,663,000 of small fry have been sent out from the piscicultural establishment at Tadousac, and these have been deposited in twenty rivers.

Such is the simple method employed in the artificial reproduction of salmon.

The destruction of fish in the water courses and lakes of Canada, which formerly teemed with them, was progressing rapidly, owing to the unintelligent way in which fishing was carried on, but by the aid of pisciculture the fish that have been destroyed will now be replaced.

The art of artificial breeding is still in its infancy, it would appear, and most marvellous results may be accomplished later on. The crossing of different species is being studied. The eggs of trout have been successfully fecundated with the milt of salmon and salmon eggs with the milt from trout and it is ascertained that species may be varied indefinitely so long as only fish of the same family are operated on.

Lord Dufferin, Governor General of Canada, whose favorite resort was Tadousac, wished to have experiments made with the *ouananish*, the famous Lake St John salmon. Unfortunately the messengers sent by him at great expense to those shores in search of specimens of this royal inhabitant of the inland sea, did not know how to manage. They arrived in the Lake region when the *ouananish* had already ascended the rivers for milting and never thought of following them. Lord Dufferin had disbursed 500 dollars for this expedition which produced no favorable result.

The Governor's idea was a good one. The *ouananish*, which only frequents fresh water, has not as highly colored flesh nor so savory a flavor as the congenerous salmon, which passes freely from the salt water into the running rivers. Crossing the breed might improve it.

Besides there was another reason and a better one; the *ouananish* is excellent eating for the colonists established on the shores of Lake St John. An abuse is made of fishing for it, particularly since so many sportsmen have been brought to these shores by means of the railroad and the fish may become extinct or nearly so. Why should it not be artificially bred at Tadousac in the same way as the salt-water salmon?

This was Lord Dufferin's way of thinking and he was in the right.

Although Tadousac is the principal centre of salmon reproduction, and the official superintendent place a certain amount of young fry in the lake which feeds their artificial streams, that is not the place where sportsmen congregate for fishing. They penetrate further to the rivers where salmon abounds. At Tadousac the young salmon grow in peace until they are twelve or fourteen inches long, then they leap over the sluices, cross the pond of the breeding-fish and gain the sea. Fishing for them in the reserved lake is not allowed, but when once they are in the sea, whoever can may take them. At this young age they take the fly as readily as **their** fathers and mothers. But this is poor sport, only fit for novices in the art, and cannot be compared with the excitement of veteran fishermen when in the wild passes of the Ste Marguerite **or the Manicouagan**, they feel a large fish at the end **of their** line and find work for their wrist and opportunity of showing their skill.

Does this mean that on the shores of **Tadousac**, fishermen in slippers may be met with amusing themselves by massacreing inoffensive loaches as at Kamouraska, or ignoble hog-fish as at Rimouski ?

No, Tadousac fish-hooks are **not baited for** such small fry ; they are destined **for more** dignified exploits and we **will try to** describe some of them.

The principal **and** most interesting sport is fishing for sea-trout in the waters of the Saguenay, at about three miles down stream from Tadousac. Sometimes even they may be caught on the very shore, in the Bay. But during the months of June and July, they particularly favor the extremity of the rocky point separating the Bay of Tadousac in two, called l'Islet by the people of the place ; they also frequent the banks along the left coast, Basque Cove, Pointe à la Croix, Laboule Cove, Passe-Pierre Islets. On the right bank they may chiefly be found at Anse à David, Pointe Noire, Catharine Bay and towards Isle aux Morts. All who are armed with patience and with lines know these privileged spots, which can be visited one after the other in less than an hour in a barge. No fly-fisher would deny himself the pleasure of breakfasting on a trout weighing not less than from two to five pounds. For those who prefer longer fishing excursions splendid sea-trout fishing is to be had at the Little Bergeronnes river, which rolls its swift waters into the St Lawrence about twelve miles below Tadousac. This place can be reached either in a yacht or barge, as likewise by land, or by the sea way, and the fishing is excellent for about three months.

The last way there which we have indicated is three miles longer and very fatiguing, but very safe for those who, though loving fishing, fear the sea.

The peaks which surround Tadousac have myriads of picturesque little fishing lakes hidden away on their sides, where enormous quantities of fish may be taken. We will mention the principal ones.

At less than a mile's distance, on the heights, we come first to lake Tadousac.

A barge will take you in an hour's run, to the pretty Laboule pond. Trout abound there in August and September. A path of a mile's length separates it from the Saguenay. Those in whom the line and the fly have not entirely destroyed all taste for things of this world may pause for an instant in the little sandy cove sheltered by Cape Laboule. In 1690, when Phipps came to besiege Quebec, it was there that three French vessels, laden with money for the troops and other royal property, sought a place of safety. The crew buried on the shore four or five thousand livres of specie and landed a battery of cannon to defend them. When the enemy, on returning from their expedition, arrived opposite the Saguenay, they suspected that the French vessels were hidden there and they attempted to enter the river, but they were driven back into the offing by the currents. Two days afterwards the French vessels came out from their place of retreat. Do not spend your time in searching for this money on the shore, as so many treasure-seekers have been doing since that memorable date, for the French vessels safely carried to Quebec the specie which they had buried!

Lakes Paradis, Sapin, Thomas, Gobeil, François, Fontaine are reputed in this district to be famous fishing-places. They can be reached in a conveyance or on foot. If possessed of a moderate amount of skill in the management of the line, trout may be caught from ten to twenty-five inches long and weighing sometimes as much as six pounds.

On returning from these excursions, ye melancholy and unsuccessful fishermen, who have only withdrawn your line from the water to change the gentle on your hook, seat yourselves on the shore and console yourselves by gazing into the offing at the sea-gulls which are skimming over the limpid water. See how they manage to catch the fish that are so shy of your hooks! After having hovered a moment with their wings motionless, they suddenly plunge into the water and emerge from it with a streak of silver in their beaks. But hasten home if they only skim the water in their headlong course, for it is a sign of approaching storm. It is a barometer far surpassing those made by the most skilful hands.

Champlain recounts enthusiastically that on Lark Point, that far stretching peninsula, " covered with large-leaved parsley and wild peas, with all sorts of shells, &c ", there was so much game, " such an abundance of wild ducks, teal, wild geese as well as larks, curlews, thrushes, woodcocks ", that on some days three or four hunters would kill more than 300 dozen head, and this game proved fat and very delicate eating.

In 1629 when Kertk took him to Tadousac as a prisoner of war, Champlain took pleasure in accompanying his conqueror to the chase. He assures us that, during the twelve days he remained there, more than 20,000 larks, plovers, curlews and snipes were killed.

Certainly sportsmen of the present day can not boast of such phenomenal hecatombs. No matter, there is still sport to be had at Tadousac. In the autumn, the local Nimrods kill divers, but in summer they bring down black duck, pigeons, magpies, larks, ospreys. In the neighborhood of the lakes the shy and timid partridge often falls a victim to fishermen who have been disheartened by their want of success at sea. It is said that ptarmigan formerly abounded at Lark Point. Father Le Jeune relates, when he landed to say Mass at Tadousac in the month of June, 1632, a soldier killed a large eagle near its eyrie. The head and neck of this bird were white, its beak and feet yellow, the rest of its body blackish, and it was as large as a turkey-cock.

In the course of the autumn the Tadousac people shoot the *beescies*, pigeons, *takaouis* and large wild geese, flocks of which fly in an angular mass, looking like a black rent in the pearly-grey sky.

There is no country so uninhabitable as this, writes Charlevoix, gazing on the barren hills and desolate banks which surround Tadousac, and yet those who have planted their tents here seem to like it.

—We are not rich, said one day a good fellow who was accompanying us in our excursions, but there is not a single beggar among us. Every one can gain his livelihood in some way or other.

—Yes, things are well enough in summer; tourists bring you in money. A little suffices you. Their coming among you gives you an easy, joyous time, even if it does not bring you abundance. But, in winter, the long terrible winter, what can you do with yourselves in this solitude ?

—Oh ! in the winter, Sir, some of us navigate, keeping along the shore, cutting firewood for selling to the people on the south shore, others of us, the greater number, go into the forests and work in the *shanties* (chantiers) (1) ; a score or so of us, coming of families who from father to son have always been fishermen, remain at Tadousac to hunt the seals.

It is in that way that we pay our debts and earn enough to buy our seed-grain. Do not fancy that visitors alone would put bread in our mouths !

Whilst at Montreal and Quebec you see your lovely river imprisoned in ice bands, here it is always blue and limpid. We can go about in our canoes as in summer time. The largest frigates could anchor safely here in the very heart of the winter.

---

(1) *Chantiers* or shanties are rough little winter settlements in the woods, for cutting down timber.

When the water is calm we venture in our canoes, as far as the offing and it is there that the seals love to congregate among the currents formed by the Vaches reef, the Islet aux Morts, and the Red Island. There are some of these animals, however, who prefer the rocky reefs near the beach. It is about All Saints that seal-hunting begins. The first to arrive are the *grosse-têtes*. In another month the *brasseurs* replace them up to the middle of May. Then the *grosse-têtes* return and remain through May. When these two sorts have left us to go down the Gulf for breeding, as we are told, the more sensible seals come to pass the summer with us. These are they whom you may have seen sunning themselves on the shore when the tide is low. And then, every year, the same thing is repeated at the same epoch.

We are twenty-five seal-hunters here. Two men get into a canoe and go out to the offing. They must be men who are skilful with their oars, for the currents are swift, and floes of ice sometimes float down on us that might upset us. Whilst one man is steering at the stern the other who is standing at the bow takes aim at the seal's head, and then finishes killing it with the harpoon Formerly a good hunter made use of the harpoon only in killing the seal, as is still the practice in killing porpoises, but the seals are getting more shy and unapproachable, so the gun is preferable. A good shot is worth four dollars. We sell the skin for from one to three dollars according to its beauty. Of the rest of the animal we make oil, which is also valuable. At one time we sold it fifty cents a gallon, but now it is only thirty-five cents, the times being bad. In the winter a canoe can bring to land from three to six seals at each expedition ; in summer sometimes as many as ten seals are killed between sunrise and sunset.

The good hunter keeps the shoulder and breast of the seal as choice morsels. The tongue, flappers and heart are also much appreciated as food. Some cooks excel in their way of preparing this meat. After having soaked it for a day in cold water and then scalded it, it is well roasted with slices of salt pork. The taste of it seems strange at first, but one gets accustomed to it. One eats worse things than that in towns.

With these words, our hunter wound up his recital.

On listening to this brave man's conversation we could not help thinking of the old days when its hunting and fishing had spread afar the fame of Tadousac and had, as it were, won for it the name of being one of the principal commercial centres of all America.

Tadousac now possesses twenty-five hunters, whereas three centuries ago the Basque vessels which thronged thither for whale-fishing were innumerable. At this present day when one of these cetaceous monsters happens to make its appearance on these shores, the newspapers speak of the occurrence for many months.

In one single week in 1650, Couillard de Lespinay killed 220 seals at Red Island (1), the same number as are now taken in a whole

---

(1) Journal of the Jesuits, p. 263.

winter. In one day at Murray Bay he caught a million cod-fish (1).

Lastly, long before a contemporary engineer proposed to go and hunt the seal in the Gulf by the aid of cannon, revolver and mitrailleuse, a Frenchman named Hilaire Brideau had tried the same weapons with whales. In 1733 (2), the Intendant of Canada gave him permission to hunt whales from Hare Island as far as Manicouagan, on both shores of the river, with a fishing boat, built in the Biscay fashion, manned by eight sailors and having on board a cannon carrying balls of two or three pounds' calibre, harpoons and 400 fathoms of cable. All stranded whales bearing the marks of harpoons or balls were to be looked on as belonging to him. Now or never can we say with Virgil :

Omnia jam vulgata............................
....
..tentanda via est, qua me quoque possim
Tollere humo, victorque virum volitare per ora.

---

(1) Id. p. 200.
(2) *Ordonnance* of March 17th, vol. 21, Intendants' Registers.

END.

TABLE OF CONTENTS

I

                                                          PAGE

Arrival by night.—First sight of Tadousac.—**The Mamelons.**—Origin of the word Tadousac.—L'Anse à l'Eau 5

II

Why Tadousac is not a **large city.**—The Indians of prehistoric times 17

III

Jacques-Cartier.—The establishment founded by Champlain.—The Court of King Petault.—Champlain.—The Basques, hardy seamen.—Their smuggling trade 28

IV

Champlain meets the Indians.—How an unfortunate **alliance** grew **out** of a visit of courtesy.—The founder of the colony as a theologian.—The first one to break his pipe.—The brothers Kertk.—**The death** of Captain **Daniel** at Tadousac.—His funeral 42

V

The Tadousac trading. — Trading post. — Of the king's farming out of the trading and the sub-farmers. — Surveyor Normandin's explorations 62

VI

The Tadousac missionaries. — Huguenots and Catholics. — Recollets and Jesuits. — One hundred and sixty-seven years of apostleship. — 1615-1782 77

VII

Explorations of the Jesuit missionaries. — Their diplomacy. — How they became valuable auxiliaries to the government. 111

VIII

Of the primitive Saguenay churches. — The Tadousac chapel .. 137

IX

Father de la Brosse. — History and legends 168

X

What has become of the aborigenes. — The doom of Mamelons. — What modern Tadousac is like. — The ambition of the Tadousacians. — Seaport and winter navigation. — Sea bathing and tourists. — A walk around the neighborhood of Tadousac. — The encroaching sands. — Fatalism. — The Baude mill and its marbles. 204

XI

Hunting and fishing. – Ichthyological establishment. – Artificial salmon-breeding. – Sea-trout. – Fishing in the **lakes**. – Seal-fishing 227

END.

www.ingramcontent.com/pod-product-compliance
Lightning Source LLC
Chambersburg PA
CBHW020800230426
43666CB00007B/785